# Leap Motion
# for Developers

Abhishek Nandy

Apress®

*Leap Motion for Developers*

Abhishek Nandy
Kolkata, West Bengal
India

ISBN-13 (pbk): 978-1-4842-2549-3          ISBN-13 (electronic): 978-1-4842-2550-9
DOI 10.1007/978-1-4842-2550-9

Library of Congress Control Number: 2016961313

Distributed to the book trade worldwide by Springer Science+Business Media New York, 233 Spring Street, 6th Floor, New York, NY 10013. Phone 1-800-SPRINGER, fax (201) 348-4505, e-mail orders-ny@springer-sbm.com, or visit www.springeronline.com. Apress Media, LLC is a California LLC and the sole member (owner) is Springer Science + Business Media Finance Inc (SSBM Finance Inc). SSBM Finance Inc is a **Delaware** corporation.

For information on translations, please e-mail rights@apress.com, or visit www.apress.com.

Apress and friends of ED books may be purchased in bulk for academic, corporate, or promotional use. eBook versions and licenses are also available for most titles. For more information, reference our Special Bulk Sales–eBook Licensing web page at www.apress.com/bulk-sales.

Any source code or other supplementary materials referenced by the author in this text are available to readers at www.apress.com. For detailed information about how to locate your book's source code, go to www.apress.com/source-code/. Readers can also access source code at SpringerLink in the Supplementary Material section for each chapter.

Printed on acid-free paper

*This book is dedicated to my Mom and Dad.*

# Contents at a Glance

# Contents

# About the Author

**Abhishek Nandy** is the second individual from India to get the prestigious Intel Black Belt Developer (https://software.intel.com/en-us/blackbelt), Microsoft MVP (https://mvp.microsoft.com/en-us/PublicProfile/5001400?fullName=Abhishek%20%20Nandy), and Intel Software Innovator (https://software.intel.com/en-us/intel-software-innovators/meet-innovators).

He writes at CodeProject(http://www.codeproject.com/Articles/Abhishek-Nandy/). He is also Featured Developer at Devmesh Intel Site (https://devmesh.intel.com/). Abhishek has proposed two whitepapers for Intel (*RealSense with Windows UAP* and *Windows 10UWP Integration*). His startup was among the top 50 at both the Digital India Innovate Challenge and Intel's IoT Ultimate Coder Challenge. He can be contacted at abhishek.nandy81@gmail.com. Youtube channel: https://www.youtube.com/channel/ucd1ibc7l6qnppnmyjubi0tg.

He is the founder of Geek Monkey Studios.

# About the Technical Reviewer

**Sumitra Bagchi** has completed a Masters in Computer Application and worked in web development and software development for more than six years before working as an individual contributor for the last three years. Her current focus is in Docker, PHP7, IOT, Xamarin, and IBM Bluemix.

She has won worldwide Spiceworks challenges and also won honourable mention at the worldwide FLIR camera hackathon. She also worked with Windows 365 development projects.

She is a premium instructor for Udemy online tutorial.

# Acknowledgments

To my mom, dad, my brother, Debashree Chanda(co-author). To the entire Intel Software Innovator Team,I ntel Black Team,Microsoft MVP community. Especially to Bob Duffy who just showed me the path to contribute to Intel, Ujjwal Kumar, Abhishek Narain, my friend Sourav Lahoti, and one of my fellow innovators Rupam Das, as well as the CEO of Platino Peach Icaza Pellen and also the CEO of Black Gate Games John Gould.

—Abhishek Nandy

To Peach Icaza Pellen, whom I admire a lot. I like the way she has become so well-known in the game developer community, and I would like to follow in her footsteps.

—Debashree Chanda

# CHAPTER 1

■ ■ ■

# Introduction to Leap Motion

This book is dedicated to showing how Leap Motion works and the different programming languages that support Leap Motion, along with the interaction techniques they use. We will provide a full guide to getting started with Leap Motion development with Unreal 4.13 (the latest update when this book was written) and also with Unity. In this book we first introduce the Leap Motion Controller, or sensor, and then look at the different Leap Motion versions. This book will cover of the extensive programming language support for Leap Motion Controller.

In this chapter we will cover the basics of Leap Motion and introduce the device. Then we will discuss why it is useful, and introduce the different gestures supported in Leap Motion. Finally, we'll note the variants of Leap Motion covered.

## Basics of Leap Motion

Leap Motion Controller is a device that is one of a kind, as it is in the first generation of touchess computing. The core capability of the device is detecting finger and hand movement and generating spatial coordinates you can use in VR game development.

The sensor is a hardware device that you attach to your computer via USB cable (see Figure 1-1).

**Electronic supplementary material** The online version of this chapter (doi:10.1007/978-1-4842-2550-9_1) contains supplementary material, which is available to authorized users.

*Figure 1-1.* *Leap Motion device with USB*

The Leap Motion device looks like Figure 1-2.

*Figure 1-2.* *Leap Motion device*

You can see how small the device is, but it is very powerful as it detects hand and finger sensor movement very easily and very precisely.

# Axis Capability

Let's take look at the axis capability of the Leap sensor.

The most important part of learning to work with Leap Motion is getting a feel for how the coordinates work. The coordinates are fully supported in three dimensions; that is, the X, Y, and Z axes.

The working of coordinates is shown in Figure 1-3.

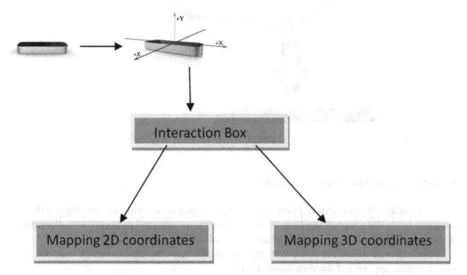

*Figure 1-3. Coordinate mapping of Leap Motion*

The Leap Motion controller is at the center of reference. The origin of Leap Motion coordinates is located at the top-center of the sensor (see Figure 1-4).

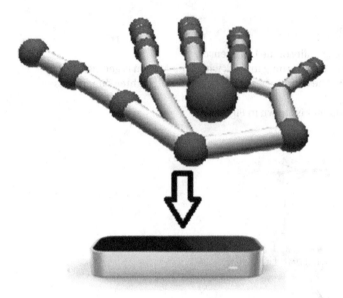

**Figure 1-4.** *Leap Motion origin of center*

For any application you're planning, you have to see which coordinate values will work the best. The range of the Leap Motion sensor is an inverted pyramid, with the point of the inverted pyramid originating at the center of the Leap Motion sensor.

The interaction box creates a rectangular area for the Leap Motion range that can be used for your app, called the *rectilinear area*.

To map coordinates for 2D and 3D, you must first normalize the points that needs to be mapped. The normalized values that we obtain are useful for determining the range. Multiplication plays a vital role in adjusting the accessibility of an application. Listing 1-1 shows how mapping is done in 2D; this is just default code.

**Listing 1-1.** The Default Code for Mapping in 2D in C#

```
int appWidth = 800;
int appHeight = 600;

InteractionBox iBox = leap.Frame().InteractionBox;
if(leap.Frame().Hands.Count > 0){
  Hand hand = leap.Frame().Hands[0];
  Finger finger = hand.Fingers[1];

  Leap.Vector leapPoint = finger.StabilizedTipPosition;
  Leap.Vector normalizedPoint = iBox.NormalizePoint(leapPoint, false);

  float appX = normalizedPoint.x * appWidth;
  float appY = (1 - normalizedPoint.y) * appHeight;
  //The z-coordinate is not used
}
```

You can see in the sample code that first we declare the range with a height and width. Then we declare the interaction box as shown, read the Hand and Finger values, and finally normalize the interaction box point range.

The next code example shows how we do mapping in three dimensions. In the first example we didn't use the Z-axis, as we were working in 2D. We need more information when we are using 3D mapping, as first we need to decide which hand rule is applied, the left-hand rule or the right-hand rule, and then we will have to scale the values accordingly. Let's check the default code in Listing 1-2.

***Listing 1-2.*** 3D Mapping for Coordinates

```
Leap.Vector leapToWorld(Leap.Vector leapPoint, InteractionBox iBox)
{
    leapPoint.z *= -1.0f; //right-hand to left-hand rule
    Leap.Vector normalized = iBox.NormalizePoint(leapPoint, false);
    normalized += new Leap.Vector(0.5f, 0f, 0.5f); //recenter origin
    return normalized * 100.0f; //scale
}
```

The code above scales the interaction box to 200 3d units.

3D mapping is essential if we want to work in free space. If we intend to make our application more intuitive and useful, we have to manage the interaction box and its coordinates precisely. When we see sample applications from the store (Leap Motion App Home), we find that the apps are managed well in free space. The accessibility of hands in free space is very important (see Figure 1-5).

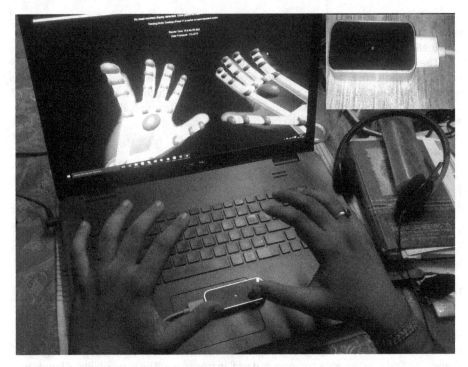

*Figure 1-5.* *Managing hands in free space*

# Motion-Tracking Capabilities of Leap Motion

Motion tracking is a very important term in the context of Leap Motion. Figure 1-6 shows the 3D and 2D space capabilities that have been defined in terms of the Leap Motion sensor's range.

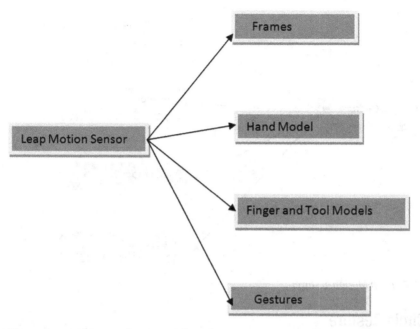

*Figure 1-6.* *Motion tracking capability of Leap Motion Controller*

# Frames

The Frame object describes the overall motion as depicted by the Leap Motion sensor's range. It adds logic to the working principles of Leap Motion.

# The Hand Model

The hand model provides information about the position, characteristics, and movement of a detected hand, including a list of fingers and tools associated with the hand.

# The Finger and Tool Model

The art of using fingers for Leap Motion Controller activity is captured by fingers and tools using one of three lists: Pointables, Fingers, and Tools.

# Gestures

The Leap Motion sensor is designed to recognize some predefined gestures and captures the data frame accordingly (see Figure 1-7).

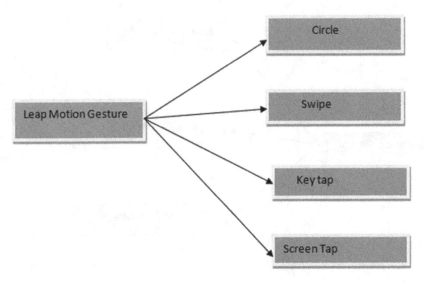

*Figure 1-7.* *Leap Motion gestures*

## The Circle Gesture

Figure 1-8 illustrates a finger creating a *circle* gesture. The circle gesture with Leap Motion can be performed by fingers on both the left and right hands.

*Figure 1-8.* *The Circle gesture*

## The Swipe Gesture

Linear movement of the hand or finger is known as a *swipe* gesture (Figure 1-9). Swipes can be of four types: up, down, left, and right.

***Figure 1-9.*** *The Swipe gesture*

## The Key Tap Gesture

The Leap sensor recognizes a tapping gesture of a finger on a key, which it logically calls the *key tap* gesture (Figure 1-10).

***Figure 1-10.*** *The keytap gesture*

## The Screentap Gesture

The Leap Motion sensor also recognizes the gesture of quickly tapping its screen as a movement (Figure 1-11).

*Figure 1-11.* *The Screentap gesture*

# Leap Motion Types

The Leap Motion sensor has undergone changes since its first release. It has gone one stop farther with introduction of the Orion unit (its Virtual Reality offset). This book will generally cover the earlier version of the Leap Motion device, V2. We will be using the new SDK, which integrates support for Orion VR but also works with the earlier version of Leap Motion.

You will download the new SDK in Chapter 2; you'll see that it comes with Orion features integrated; although we can use it with Leap Motion V2, too, it is perfect with Orion.

The Leap Motion website (`https://www.leapmotion.com/`) now reflects the Orion version (Figure 1-12).

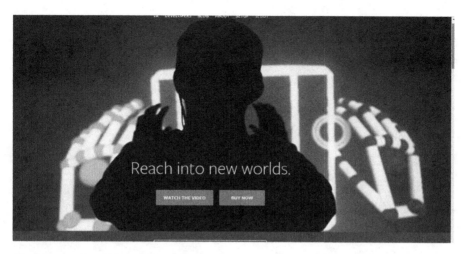

***Figure 1-12.*** *Leap Motion Orion VR*

Orion is part hardware and part software, which allows very easy hand tracking techniques for VR apps. It works on lower latency, which allows a longer range.

Orion currently supports the following VR devices:

- Oculus Rift DK2

- Oculus Rift CV1

- HTC Vive

# Summary

In this chapter we introduced the Leap Motion Controller and the types that are available right now. We also gave an overview of the spatial range controlled by Leap Motion. Finally, we introduced Leap Motion's Orion Beta.

# CHAPTER 2

■ ■ ■

# Setting Up Leap Motion

In the previous chapter we introduced you to some basics of the Leap Motion sensor and the different hardware updates to it. In this chapter we will go through the details of setting up the Leap Motion for Windows SDK, starting with where to get the SDK.

The chapter will start with the Leap Motion website (`https://www.leapmotion.com/`), where you can find all the details to get started. From the link there we will install the Leap Motion and Orion SDK. When installation is done we will review the tools on the Leap Motion SDK Control Panel. Then we will briefly look at where to find additional software available for the SDK to expand the capabilities of Leap Motion.

## Downloading the Leap Motion SDK

We will start with what the website for Leap Motion looks like and then explore the important information within the site. Let's take a look at the landing page (Figure 2-1).

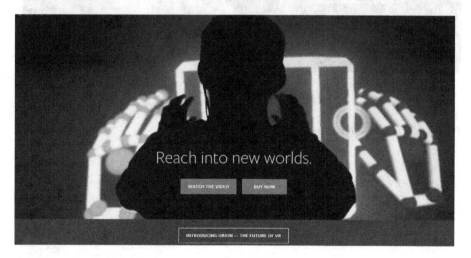

***Figure 2-1.*** *Leap Motion website*

© Abhishek Nandy 2016
A. Nandy, *Leap Motion for Developers*, DOI 10.1007/978-1-4842-2550-9_2

In the main page for Leap Motion you can see two links to start; with one is Watch the Video and the other is Buy Now (Figure 2-2). The Watch the Video link will show a demo on how Leap Motion Orion works; the Buy Now link will take us to a page where we can purchase the Leap Motion sensor.

***Figure 2-2.*** *Introducing Orion option in website*

The next section of the website gives details about Leap Motion Orion.

Clicking Introducing Orion-The Future Of VR will take you to a page with information about Orion (`https://developer.leapmotion.com/orion`). Here you can click Download the Beta (Figure 2-3).

***Figure 2-3.*** *Information about Orion Beta*

The Orion Beta page gives a lot of information about the usage of the Beta SDK. When you choose Download Beta, it will take you to the page where we can download the Orion Beta SDK (Figure 2-4).

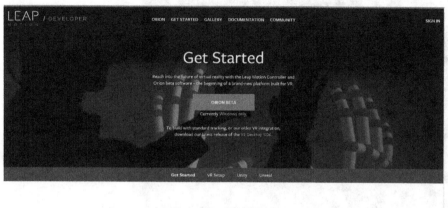

*Figure 2-4. Orion Beta download link*

As you've seen on the website, the focus of the Leap Motion sensor is shifting more toward VR with its latest release of the Orion SDK. In the next section you'll see how to install the SDK for Leap Motion.

# Installing the Leap Motion SDK

Unpack the Leap Motion sensor and attach it with a USB cable to your PC or laptop as shown in Figure 2-5.

***Figure 2-5.*** *Leap Motion Controller attached*

You will see an information screen where you'll be directed to a link (https://www. leapmotion.com/setup, shown in Figure 2-6).

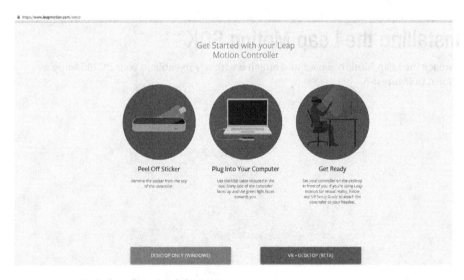

***Figure 2-6.*** *The link to download the SDK*

From here, download the setup application and then run the exe file (Figure 2-7).

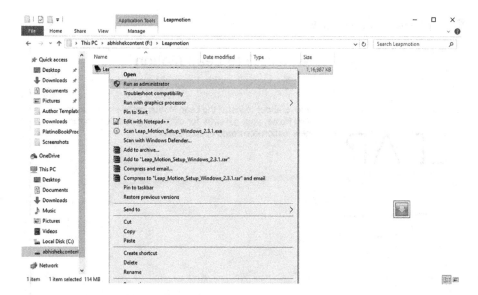

***Figure 2-7.*** *Running the setup file*

The setup will start. You need to click Next, as shown in Figure 2-8.

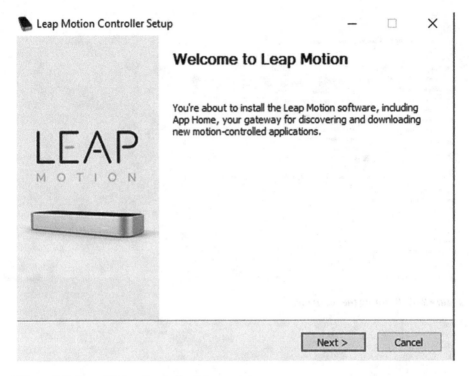

*Figure 2-8.* *Leap Motion Controller Setup opening screen*

Accept the license agreement and then click I Agree (Figure 2-9).

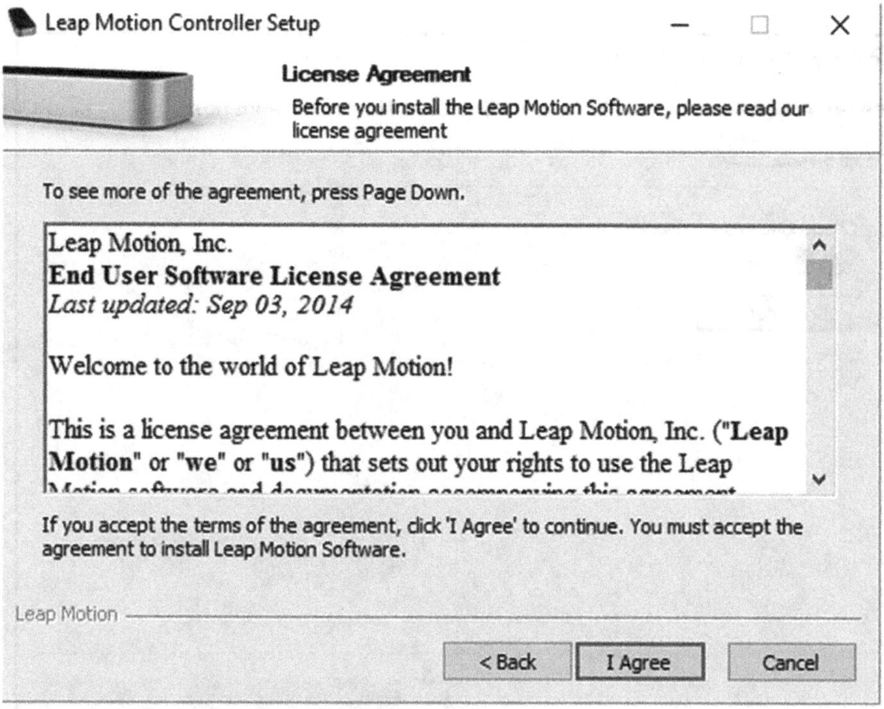

**Figure 2-9.** *Accepting the license agreement*

After the previous step Installation starts; it will go ahead and install important files (Figure 2-10).

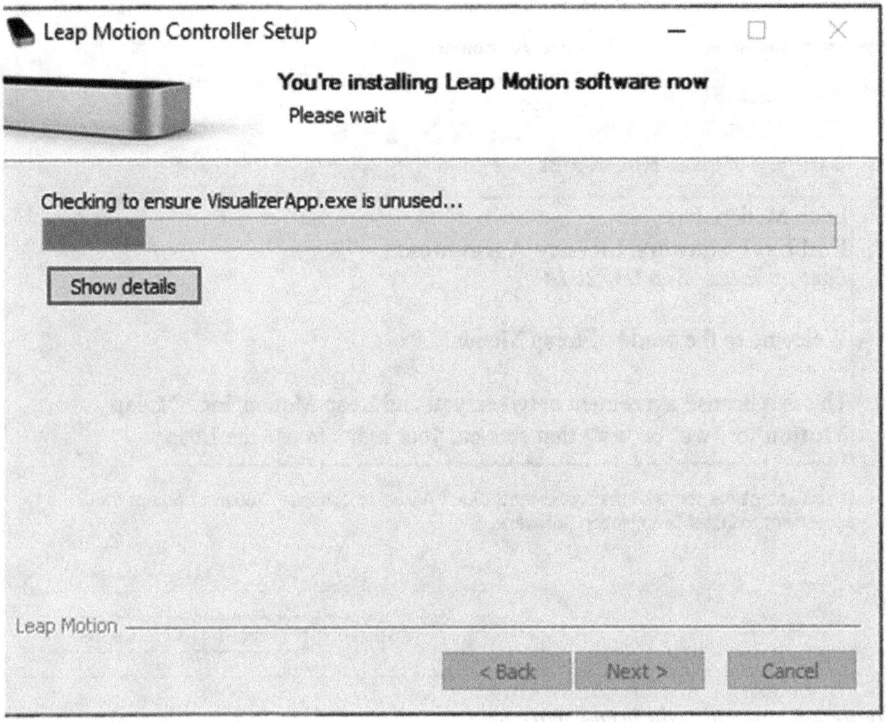

*Figure 2-10. Installation starts*

The setup program will let you know about more steps it has to follow during installation (Figure 2-11).

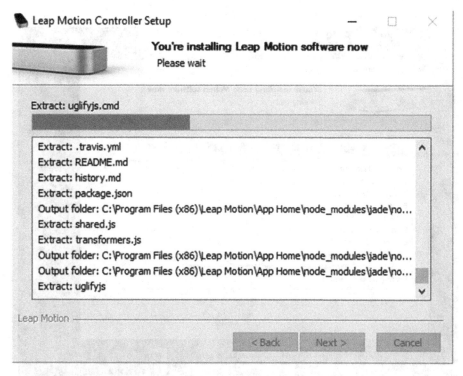

***Figure 2-11.*** *Important installations continue*

In the next step you can see that the installation is almost complete, and it will next try to install the hardware driver for the Leap Motion SDK (Figure 2-12). You need to click Install so that the Leap Motion SDK and the sensor are in sync and ready to go.

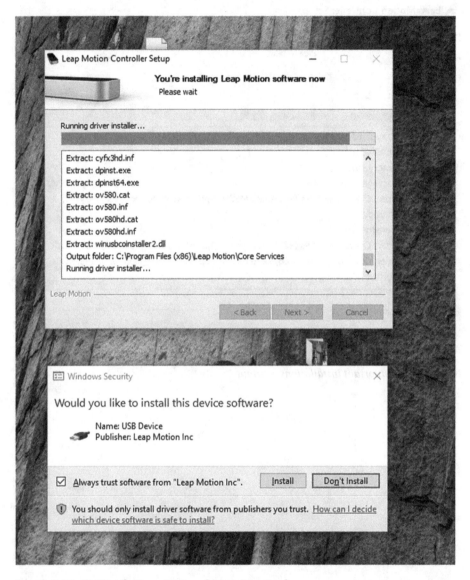

*Figure 2-12. Getting the Leap Motion device recognized*

In the final step you can see that the Leap Motion SDK is installed and you are ready to work with the Leap Motion sensor and the programming interface (Figure 2-13).

*Figure 2-13. Installation of SDK is complete*

# The Leap Motion Control Panel

We will now look at the Leap Motion Control Panel. The updated Leap Motion Control Panel is available after you install the SDK for Orion. From the system tray, right-click the Leap Motion icon and select Settings as shown in Figure 2-14.

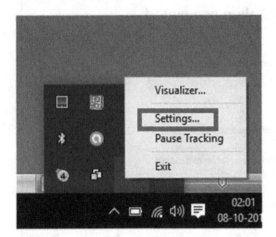

***Figure 2-14.*** *Right-click the Leap Motion icon to access Settings for Leap Motion*

In the Control Panel you can see the tabs that are useful for calibration and other important features of Leap Motion and for verifying that the Leap Motion device is working correctly.

The General tab provides important introductory information about using the Leap Motion sensor SDK. As the Leap Motion SDK and Leap Motion are being set up, you can check the progress details by recalibrating the device on the Troubleshooting tab as shown in Figure 2-15. To repeat the process, click Recalibrate Device again.

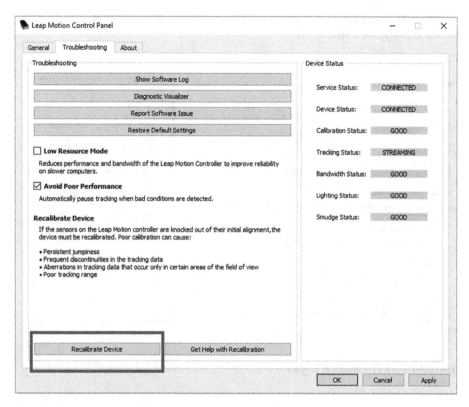

*Figure 2-15.* *We can recalibrate the device*

The calibration status is complete when you have set up the Leap Motion device for the first time (Figure 2-16).

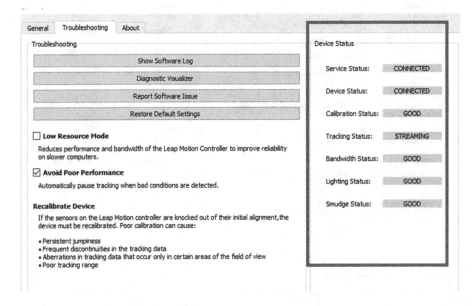

***Figure 2-16.*** *Device status is perfect*

## Software Log

Here you'll find all the information about how the Leap Motion device is working in your computer. The Software Log shows all the tracking, software updates, firmware updates as needed, and diagnostics for the device.

To display the Software Log, click the Show Software Log button, as shown in Figure 2-17. You'll then see valuable information about the device.

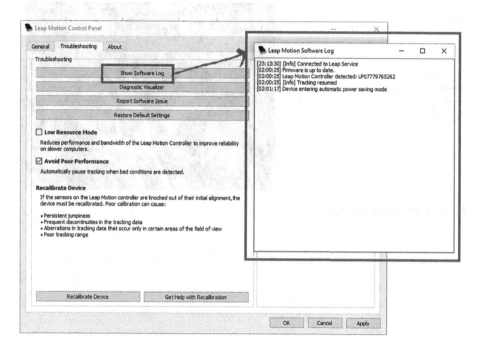

***Figure 2-17.*** *Leap Motion Software log*

## Diagnostic Visualizer

Diagnostic Visualizer gives the status of Leap Motion and its tracking ability. To use it, wave your hands in front of the Leap Motion sensor to check whether it's working (Figure 2-18).

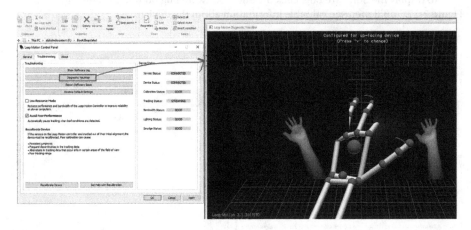

*Figure 2-18.* *Diagnostic Visualizer*

# The Calibration Tool

The next tool we'll check is the Leap Motion Calibration tool (Figure 2-19). Here you'll be instructed to point the Leap Motion at a flat reflective surface so that you can see how the Leap Motion sensor is working, with the Calibration tool. If the pass score is 80 then we have the Leap Motion working correctly. To access the tool from the Leap Control Panel, click Troubleshooting and then click Recalibrate Device to start the Calibration tool.

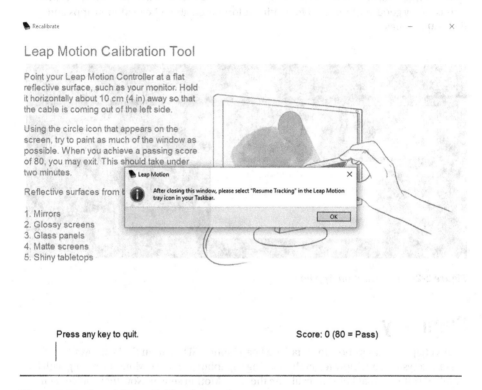

*Figure 2-19. Leap Motion Calibration tool*

29

# Leap Motion App Home

Finally, let's take a quick look at the Leap Motion App Home, for which a desktop icon is created when we install the SDK. Click the icon to start the Leap Motion App Home; when it has connected to the Internet you'll see there are a lot of good applications to explore how Leap Motion works (Figure 2-20). Here you can just search for terms like "playground," "forms," and "functioning 3D" and other options that you can select from. This is a very good starting point for getting information about Leap Motion apps and their capabilities.

***Figure 2-20.*** *Leap Motion App home*

# Summary

In this chapter you saw how to install the Leap Motion SDK within the Windows operating system, and how to get the sensing capabilities of Leap Motion working with its supplied software that helps us calibrate the Leap Motion sensor. Now that you've seen this chapter's overview of how Leap Motion SDK works, in the next chapter we will start with the programming languages.

# CHAPTER 3

■ ■ ■

# Setting Up Leap Motion for Python

In the previous chapter you saw how to install the Leap Motion SDK on a Windows computer; now we will work on setting up the Leap Motion SDK for Python. First we need to install some important Python updates that are necessary so that your Leap Motion will be recognized and you'll be able to interact with it. It's important to note that the Python installation that works with Leap Motion version v1 is Python 2.7. In this chapter we will first show you how to set up the Leap Motion for Python and then introduce some simple programs that will demonstrate how the Python language works with the Leap Motion sensor.

## Leap Motion and Python

This book's journey to developing for Leap Motion starts with the Python language. We want to show how Leap Motion works with different programming languages and how it is easy to integrate Leap Motion with different languages, so we have chosen Python to start with because it is both simple and of course very powerful.

Python is a powerful dynamic programming language that has the capability of adding object-oriented flow into the programming construct when constructing application logic. The most important thing about Python is that we can write and express our coding logic very simply, with a few lines of code. It's very easy to use Python in different operating systems. Another important fact about Python is that it is an open source language. Figure 3-1 shows how we integrate Leap Motion SDK with Python.

© Abhishek Nandy 2016                                                                                    31
A. Nandy, *Leap Motion for Developers*, DOI 10.1007/978-1-4842-2550-9_3

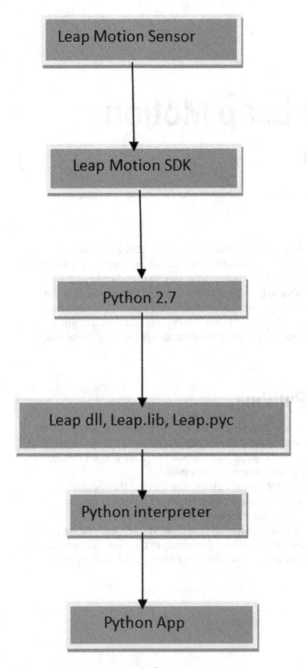

*Figure 3-1.* *Leap Motion Python App*

To get started, let's take a look at the workflow for the Leap Motion Python app.

1.  To start with, we need to be sure that the Leap Motion sensor is attached to the computer, and that the SDK for Leap Motion is installed.

2.  Because we are using the earlier version of Leap Motion, we need to be specific about the Python installation. The Python version required for this early Leap Motion is Python 2.7. You'll need to be sure that the Python 2.7 version is installed in your computer.

3.  The next step is to make a folder where you will keep your programs for Leap Motion SDK with Python.

4.  Next you have to add Python to the path of the environment variable for the computer. Once that is complete, copy the necessary DLL files into the folder that you have created.

5.  Using a text editor, you can start writing a program in Python, and as the Leap Motion SDK has all the DLL files in place, you can use the Command prompt to run the program and see its output.

This is the complete flow for Python app with Leap Motion SDK. In the next sections we'll go through each step in more detail.

# Installing Python 2.7

In this section we will install and set up Python 2.7 so that it can be used for Leap Motion SDK. We start by going to the web link to download Python 2.7 (`https://www.Python.org/downloads/release/Python-2710/`).

---

■ **Note**    You can also search on Google for Python 2.7.

---

Now we download the installer for Python 2.7 (see Figure 3-2).

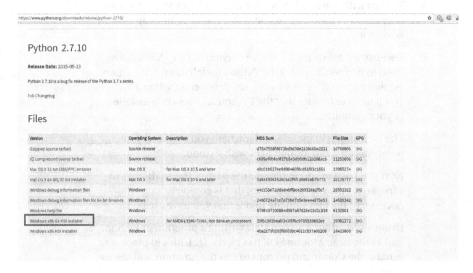

**Figure 3-2.** *Downloading the installer for Python 2.7*

Next, click Install to start the install for Python MSI package (Figure 3-3).

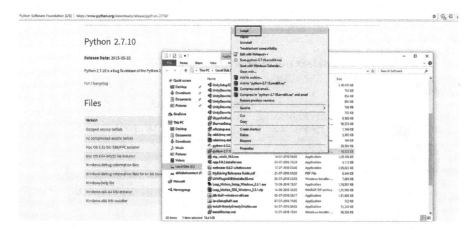

*Figure 3-3. Installing the MSI for Python 2.7*

In the next step the installation starts and you can select either Install for All Users or Install Just for Me and then click Next (Figure 3-4).

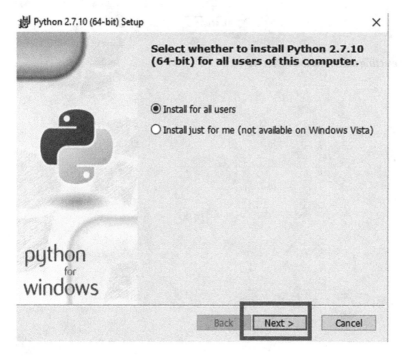

*Figure 3-4. Installing Python 2.7*

In the following step, select a destination directory for installation, and then click Next (Figure 3-5).

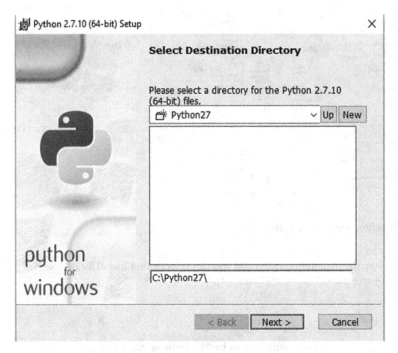

**Figure 3-5.** *Selecting a destination directory*

In the next step you can customize the installation. After customization, click Next to continue (Figure 3-6).

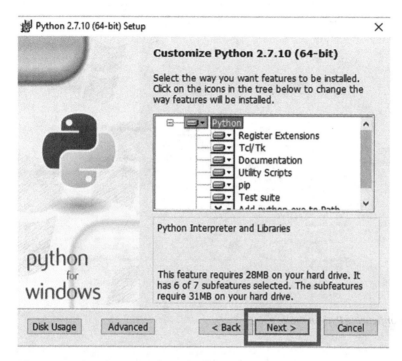

***Figure 3-6.*** *Customizing Python installation*

In the next step, Python 2.7 configures the necessary tools (Figure 3-7).

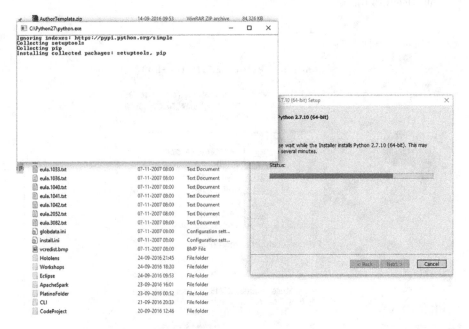

*Figure 3-7. Configuring Python tools*

In the last step you will see that the installation is complete; click Finish (Figure 3-8).

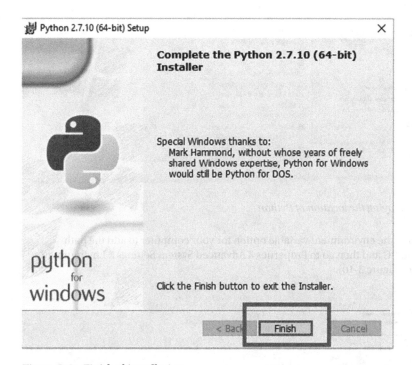

***Figure 3-8.*** *Finished installation*

# The Python Not Found Issue

Once you have installed Python 2.7, the first step is to check whether the installation and version is working or not. So open the Command Prompt and type:

```
Python --version
```

If you get an error that says

```
'Python' is not recognized as an internal or external command, operable
program or batch file.
```

The issue is that the OS environment variables for Python need to be added.

You need to copy the location of the place where you installed Python in your computer and add it to the path variable. The path needs to be copied as shown in Figure 3-9.

*Figure 3-9. Copying the location of Python*

Now go to the environment variable option for your computer to add the path. Right-click on PC and then go to Properties ä Advanced System Settings ä Environment Variables (see Figure 3-10).

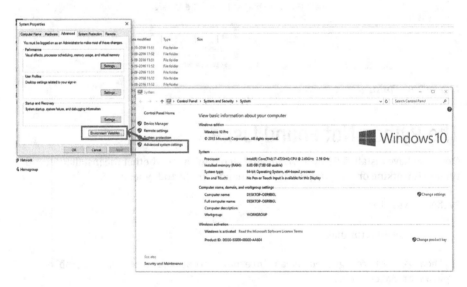

*Figure 3-10. Getting inside the environment variable option*

Now add the copied location for Python to the PATH variable and then click OK as shown in Figure 3-11.

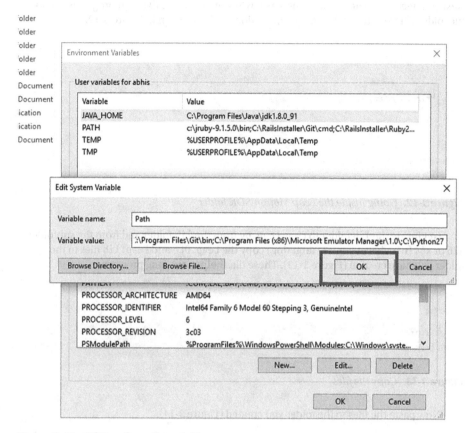

**Figure 3-11.** *Editing the path variable*

Restart the Command Prompt and you will be ready to go with Python 2.7.

# Setting Up Python for Leap Motion

Next you need to create a folder where you will store your Leap Motion programs. Go to the folder where you installed the Leap Motion SDK, as shown in Figure 3-12.

*Figure 3-12.* *Going inside the Leap Motion SDK folder*

Get inside the lib folder to copy Leap.py from the lib folder and from the subfolder x86 or x64 (whichever you are targeting) copy the Leap.DLL and Leap.lib files to the folder you have created (Figure 3-13). These files help in running programs.

| Name | Date modified | Type | Size |
|---|---|---|---|
| Leap.dll | 14-06-2016 01:19 | Application extens... | 3,553 KB |
| Leap.lib | 14-06-2016 01:19 | Object File Library | 126 KB |

*Figure 3-13.* *Copy the files*

Now paste the files to the folder you created (Figure 3-14).

*Figure 3-14.* *copying and pasting the necessary files*

You are all set now for running Python programs for the Leap Motion device.

# Setting Up the Sublime Text Editor

To write Python code, you need a text editor. Go to the website for downloading the Sublime Text editor (https://www.sublimetext.com/). Click the installer for setting up Sublime text (Figure 3-15).

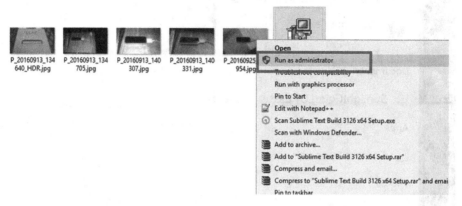

*Figure 3-15. Installing Sublime*

The wizard will go through its steps until the setup is complete (Figure 3-16).

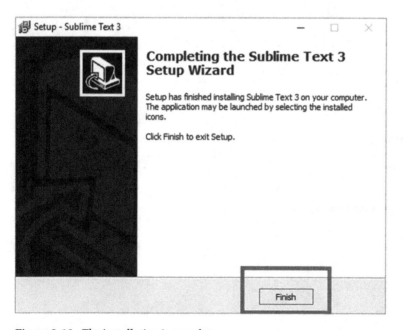

*Figure 3-16. The installation is complete*

You can now run the Sublime text program from Windows search (Figure 3-17).

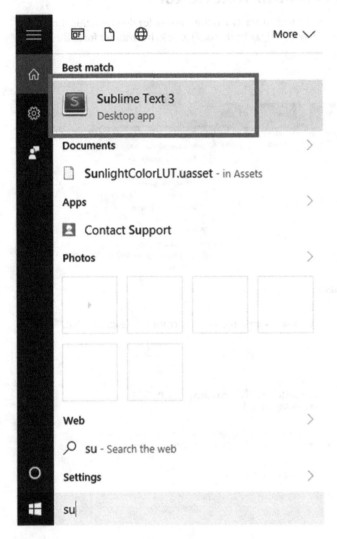

*Figure 3-17.* *Running Sublime text3*

# Let's Code

So far we have carried out the following steps to prepare for writing Python apps for Leap Motion:

1. Created a folder for storing the programs.

2. Copied the necessary DLL files for running Python programs with Leap Motion SDK.

3. Added the Python path to an environment variable.

Now we have to do three more steps:

4. Use a text editor like Sublime Text to write a program.

5. Use the Command Prompt to run the program.

6. Check the output.

## Writing a Basic Leap Motion Program

Our first program simply checks whether the Leap Motion sensor is connected or disconnected. If the user presses Enter the program exits. It is executed through the Command Prompt.

The code as run in the Sublime text editor looks like Figure 3-18, and you can see that the formatting enhances readability.

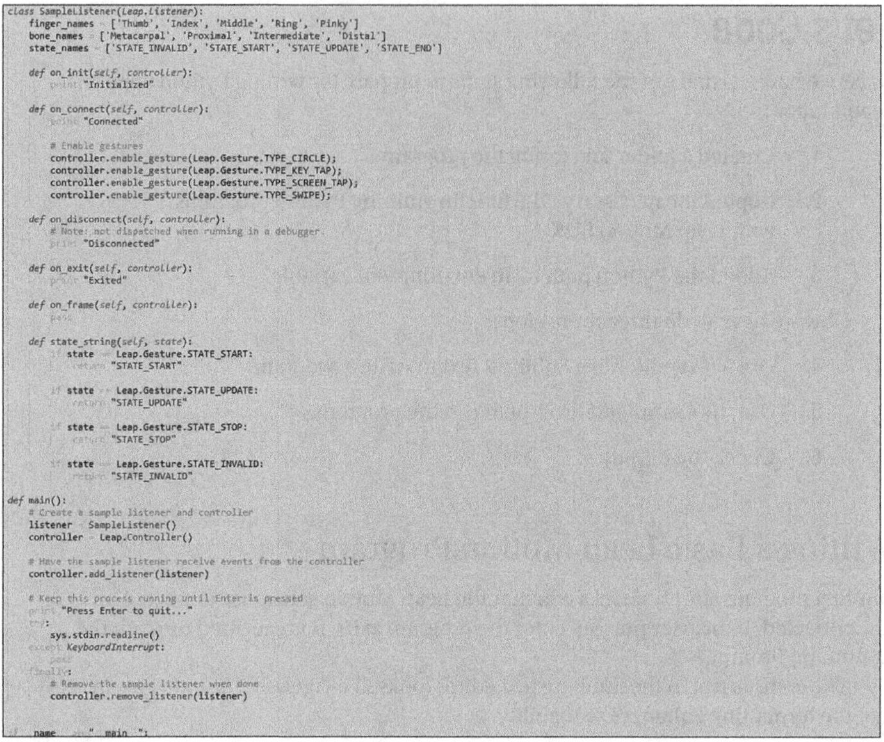

```
class SampleListener(Leap.Listener):
    finger_names = ['Thumb', 'Index', 'Middle', 'Ring', 'Pinky']
    bone_names = ['Metacarpal', 'Proximal', 'Intermediate', 'Distal']
    state_names = ['STATE_INVALID', 'STATE_START', 'STATE_UPDATE', 'STATE_END']

    def on_init(self, controller):
        print "Initialized"

    def on_connect(self, controller):
        print "Connected"

        # Enable gestures
        controller.enable_gesture(Leap.Gesture.TYPE_CIRCLE);
        controller.enable_gesture(Leap.Gesture.TYPE_KEY_TAP);
        controller.enable_gesture(Leap.Gesture.TYPE_SCREEN_TAP);
        controller.enable_gesture(Leap.Gesture.TYPE_SWIPE);

    def on_disconnect(self, controller):
        # Note: not dispatched when running in a debugger.
        print "Disconnected"

    def on_exit(self, controller):
        print "Exited"

    def on_frame(self, controller):
        pass

    def state_string(self, state):
        if state == Leap.Gesture.STATE_START:
            return "STATE_START"

        if state == Leap.Gesture.STATE_UPDATE:
            return "STATE_UPDATE"

        if state == Leap.Gesture.STATE_STOP:
            return "STATE_STOP"

        if state == Leap.Gesture.STATE_INVALID:
            return "STATE_INVALID"

def main():
    # Create a sample listener and controller
    listener = SampleListener()
    controller = Leap.Controller()

    # Have the sample listener receive events from the controller
    controller.add_listener(listener)

    # Keep this process running until Enter is pressed
    print "Press Enter to quit..."
    try:
        sys.stdin.readline()
    except KeyboardInterrupt:
        pass
    finally:
        # Remove the sample listener when done
        controller.remove_listener(listener)

if __name__ == "__main__":
```

**Figure 3-18.** *The program in Sublime Text*

Let's try to run it. Make sure you have copied all the necessary DLL files (Figure 3-19).

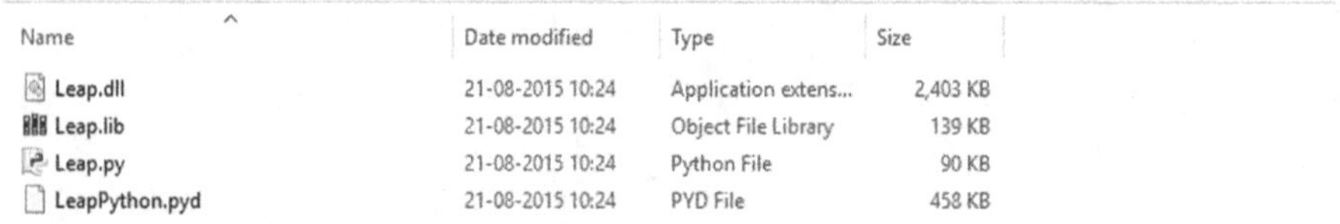

| Name ^ | Date modified | Type | Size |
|---|---|---|---|
| Leap.dll | 21-08-2015 10:24 | Application extens... | 2,403 KB |
| Leap.lib | 21-08-2015 10:24 | Object File Library | 139 KB |
| Leap.py | 21-08-2015 10:24 | Python File | 90 KB |
| LeapPython.pyd | 21-08-2015 10:24 | PYD File | 458 KB |

**Figure 3-19.** *The necessary Dll and important files*

Now you can create the file Sample1.py and open a Command Prompt to run the program.

The code for the app is shown in Listing 3-1.

*Listing 3-1.* The Code for Testing Leap Motion Controller with Python

```python
import Leap, sys, thread, time
from Leap import CircleGesture, KeyTapGesture, ScreenTapGesture,
SwipeGesture

class SampleListener(Leap.Listener):
    finger_names = ['Thumb', 'Index', 'Middle', 'Ring', 'Pinky']
    bone_names = ['Metacarpal', 'Proximal', 'Intermediate', 'Distal']
    state_names = ['STATE_INVALID', 'STATE_START', 'STATE_UPDATE', 'STATE_
    END']

    def on_init(self, controller):
        print "Initialized"

    def on_connect(self, controller):
        print "Connected"

        # Enable gestures
        controller.enable_gesture(Leap.Gesture.TYPE_CIRCLE);
        controller.enable_gesture(Leap.Gesture.TYPE_KEY_TAP);
        controller.enable_gesture(Leap.Gesture.TYPE_SCREEN_TAP);
        controller.enable_gesture(Leap.Gesture.TYPE_SWIPE);

    def on_disconnect(self, controller):
        # Note: not dispatched when running in a debugger.
        print "Disconnected"

    def on_exit(self, controller):
        print "Exited"

    def on_frame(self, controller):
        pass

    def state_string(self, state):
        if state == Leap.Gesture.STATE_START:
            return "STATE_START"

        if state == Leap.Gesture.STATE_UPDATE:
            return "STATE_UPDATE"

        if state == Leap.Gesture.STATE_STOP:
            return "STATE_STOP"
```

```
        if state == Leap.Gesture.STATE_INVALID:
            return "STATE_INVALID"

def main():
    # Create a sample listener and controller
    listener = SampleListener()
    controller = Leap.Controller()

    # Have the sample listener receive events from the controller
    controller.add_listener(listener)

    # Keep this process running until Enter is pressed
    print "Press Enter to quit..."
    try:
        sys.stdin.readline()
    except KeyboardInterrupt:
        pass
    finally:
        # Remove the sample listener when done
        controller.remove_listener(listener)

if __name__ == "__main__":
    main()
```

First go to the folder you created and copy the necessary files.

```
Microsoft Windows [Version 10.0.10586]
(c) 2015 Microsoft Corporation. All rights reserved.

C:\Users\abhis>cd\

C:\>f:

F:\>cd F:\LeapPython

F:\LeapPython>
```

Next we check the directory structure using dir (Figure 3-20). Here we run the program using the Python command with the Sample1.py file.

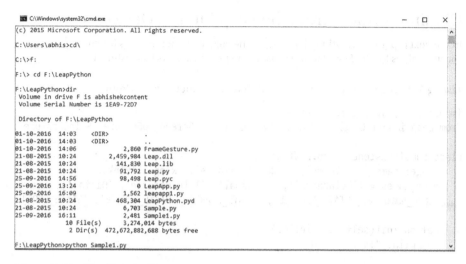

*Figure 3-20.* *Checking the files*

Check the connected and disconnected status from the PC as the program runs to verify the functionality of the app (Figure 3-21).

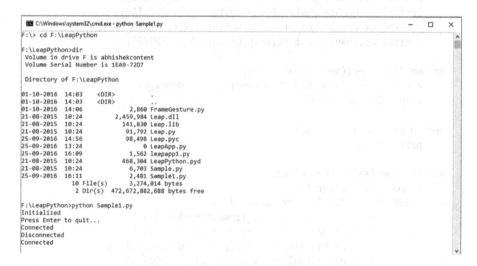

*Figure 3-21.* *Checking the functionality*

# Obtaining Values from the Leap Motion Device

In the next program everything happens in the onFrame function. This function gives specific values for the Leap Motion sensor. The program looks like Listing 3-2.

*Listing 3-2.* The Program for Accessing Different Parameter Values from Leap Motion

```
import Leap, sys, thread, time
from Leap import CircleGesture, KeyTapGesture, ScreenTapGesture, SwipeGesture

class SampleListener(Leap.Listener):
    finger_names = ['Thumb', 'Index', 'Middle', 'Ring', 'Pinky']
    bone_names = ['Metacarpal', 'Proximal', 'Intermediate', 'Distal']
    state_names = ['STATE_INVALID', 'STATE_START', 'STATE_UPDATE', 'STATE_END']

    def on_init(self, controller):
        print "Initialized"

    def on_connect(self, controller):
        print "Connected"

        # Enable gestures
        controller.enable_gesture(Leap.Gesture.TYPE_CIRCLE);
        controller.enable_gesture(Leap.Gesture.TYPE_KEY_TAP);
        controller.enable_gesture(Leap.Gesture.TYPE_SCREEN_TAP);
        controller.enable_gesture(Leap.Gesture.TYPE_SWIPE);

    def on_disconnect(self, controller):
        # Note: not dispatched when running in a debugger.
        print "Disconnected"

    def on_exit(self, controller):
        print "Exited"

    def on_frame(self, controller):
        frame = controller.frame()
        print "Frame ID: " + str(frame.id) \
                + "Timestamp: " + str(frame.timestamp) \
                + "# of Hands: " + str(len(frame.hands)) \
                + "# of Fingers: " + str(len(frame.fingers)) \
                + "# no of Tools: " + str(len(frame.tools)) \
                + "# of Gestures: " + str(len(frame.gestures())) \

    def state_string(self, state):
        if state == Leap.Gesture.STATE_START:
            return "STATE_START"
```

```python
        if state == Leap.Gesture.STATE_UPDATE:
            return "STATE_UPDATE"

        if state == Leap.Gesture.STATE_STOP:
            return "STATE_STOP"

        if state == Leap.Gesture.STATE_INVALID:
            return "STATE_INVALID"

def main():
    # Create a sample listener and controller
    listener = SampleListener()
    controller = Leap.Controller()

    # Have the sample listener receive events from the controller
    controller.add_listener(listener)

    # Keep this process running until Enter is pressed
    print "Press Enter to quit..."
    try:
        sys.stdin.readline()
    except KeyboardInterrupt:
        pass
    finally:
        # Remove the sample listener when done
        controller.remove_listener(listener)

if __name__ == "__main__":
    main()
```

The output is shown in Figure 3-22.

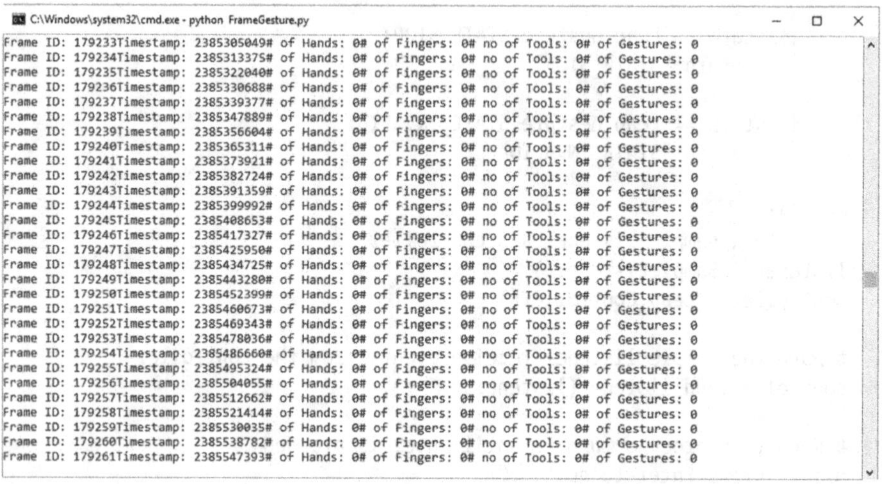

*Figure 3-22.* *The values for different sensor activities*

# Summary

In this chapter we have set up Leap Motion for the Python language. We are using Python 2.7 for our work. We also installed a text editor, in this case Sublime Text, for our work and to enhance readability of the code run via the Command Prompt.

# CHAPTER 4

■ ■ ■

# Leap Motion with Java

In the previous chapter you saw how to get started developing applications for Python using Leap Motion; now our focus will be on using the Java language. In this chapter we will start with a brief discussion of Java and then introduce the IDE that we'll use for writing Java applications, Eclipse. You will see how to download Eclipse from the link and get started with the development environment.

## A Brief Discussion of Java

We'll start with a brief overview of Java as a language. Java is a cross-platform computing language that can be extended to any operating system. The versatility of Java is such that it can be used in embedded devices as well as mobile phones and everything up to enterprise services and supercomputers, too.

Java can be extended to many applications, applets, and sandbox environments, and it can also be integrated within an HTML page. The most important part of Java is the Java Virtual Machine (JVM) specification; with the help of JVM, Java can run on many operating systems (see Figure 4-1).

© Abhishek Nandy 2016
A. Nandy, *Leap Motion for Developers*, DOI 10.1007/978-1-4842-2550-9_4

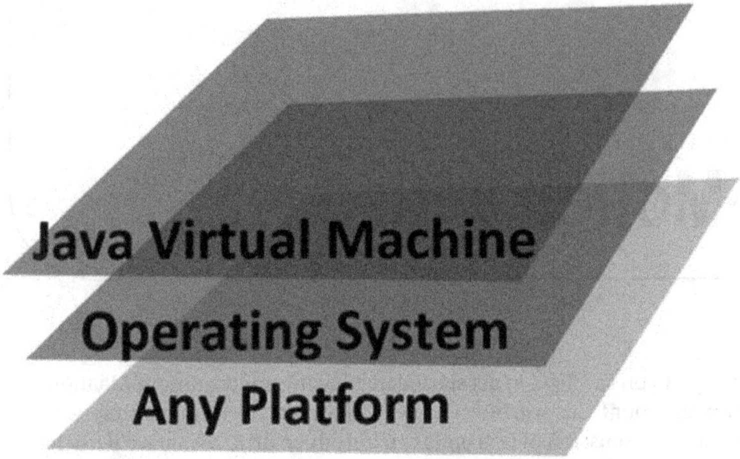

*Figure 4-1.* *how JVM helps in breaking the Java program*

Java was specifically meant to be "write once and run anywhere." Java is object-oriented, platform-independent, and architecture-neutral, as well as very portable.

In Java programs are compiled not into executable files but into *bytecode* and executed in that form. In a text editor or in Eclipse you can write a program in Java with the *.java extension; then the Java Compiler creates a *.class file and a class loader dynamically loads the Java class file to the JVM. The bytecode verifier checks the bytecode at a number of different levels. After completing the whole process, the bytecode can be consumed by any native OS. Figure 4-2 shows the entire process of how a Java program is compiled.

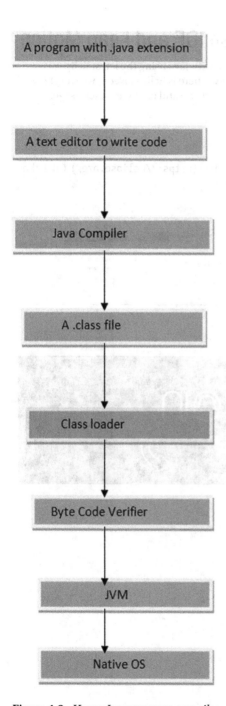

***Figure 4-2.*** *How a Java program compiles*

# Getting Started with Eclipse IDE and Leap Motion

This section shows how to integrate Leap Motion with Java using the latest Eclipse environment. The Eclipse version that we will cover here is Eclipse Neon; we will show how to download Eclipse Neon from the Eclipse website and configure it for usage.

## Installing Eclipse

Go to the link for downloading the Eclipse Neon IDE (`https://eclipse.org/`). Click the Download button to install the IDE (Figure 4-3).

***Figure 4-3.*** *Eclipse Neon download*

Now run the setup of Eclipse Neon IDE as an administrator (Figure 4-4).

| | | | | |
|---|---|---|---|---|
| Documents 📌 | 📦 rabbitmq-server-3.6.3.exe | 14-07-2016 04:56 | Application | 5,502 KB |
| Pictures 📌 | 📦 rabbitmq-dotnet-client-3.6.3-dotnet-4.5.... | 14-07-2016 04:42 | WinRAR ZIP archive | 164 KB |
| OneDrive | 🐍 python-3.5.2.exe | 06-07-2016 02:17 | Application | 28,584 KB |
| This PC | otp_win64_19.0.exe | 14-07-2016 04:36 | Application | 1,00,100 KB |
| Desktop | npp.6.9.2.Installer.exe | 29-07-2016 13:24 | Application | 4,113 KB |
| Documents | netbeans-8.0.2-windows.exe | 17-07-2016 03:49 | Application | 2,09,022 KB |
| Downloads | MyDriving Reference Guide.pdf | 21-07-2016 04:59 | PDF File | 6,444 KB |
| Music | LWAPlugin64BitInstaller32.msi | 26-07-2016 21:33 | Windows Installer ... | 7,688 KB |
| Pictures | Leap_Motion_Setup_Windows_2.3.1.exe | 13-09-2016 13:57 | Application | 1,16,987 KB |
| Videos | Leap_Motion_SDK_Windows_2.3.1.zip | 14-09-2016 10:35 | WinRAR ZIP archive | 1,51,960 KB |
| Local Disk (C:) | jdk-8u91-windows-x64.exe | 05-07-2016 02:17 | Application | 1,91,903 KB |
| abhishekcontent (F: | JavaSetup8u91.exe | 07-07-2016 15:05 | Application | 722 KB |
| | Install-G | | ion | 31,245 KB |
| Network | InstallD | **Open** | s Installer ... | 98,568 KB |
| Homegroup | Firefox-! | 🛡 Run as administrator | ion | 43,977 KB |
| | EpicGan | Troubleshoot compatibility | s Installer ... | 36,164 KB |
| | Emulato | Run with graphics processor > | ion | 1,109 KB |
| | eclipse- | Pin to Start | ion | 45,854 KB |
| | ccsetup | Edit with Notepad++ | ion | 6,832 KB |
| | BaiduBr | Scan eclipse-inst-win64.exe | ion | 1,357 KB |
| | android | Scan with Windows Defender... | ion | 12,16,417 KB |
| 42 items  1 item selected  44.7 MB | ActiveP | Open with WinRAR | ion | 35,497 KB |

*Figure 4-4. Eclipse setup*

The Eclipse Neon IDE setup will start installing (Figure 4-5).

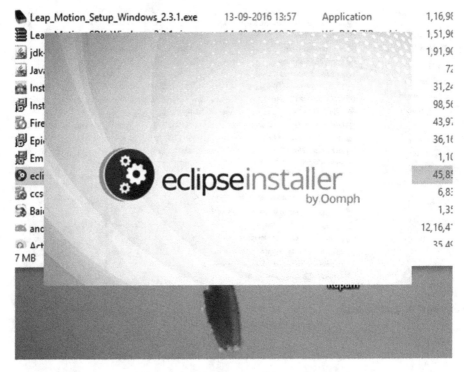

*Figure 4-5.* *Installing Eclipse Neon IDE*

Because we are going to develop for Java, select Eclipse IDE for Java Developers in the next screen (Figure 4-6). Once you've chosen this Java option, it will start installing and then configuring the Eclipse Neon IDE.

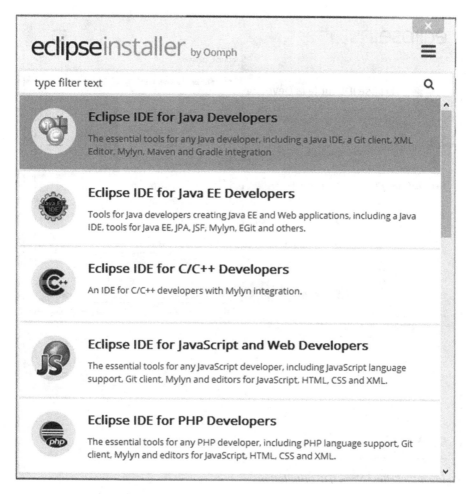

**Figure 4-6.** *Selecting the setup for Java*

Now select a folder where you will copy the installation files for the Eclipse Neon IDE. You can either choose an existing folder or create a new one (Figure 4-7).

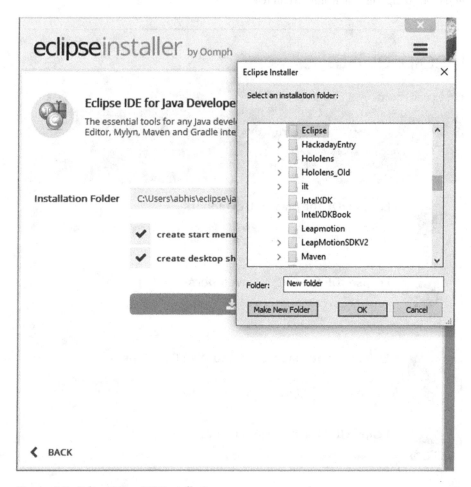

***Figure 4-7.*** *Eclipse Neon IDE installation*

You are now ready to install the Eclipse Neon IDE; click Install to get started (Figure 4-8).

*Figure 4-8.* *Click on Install*

In the next step, accept the agreement for proceeding. Once you are ready, click Accept Now (Figure 4-9).

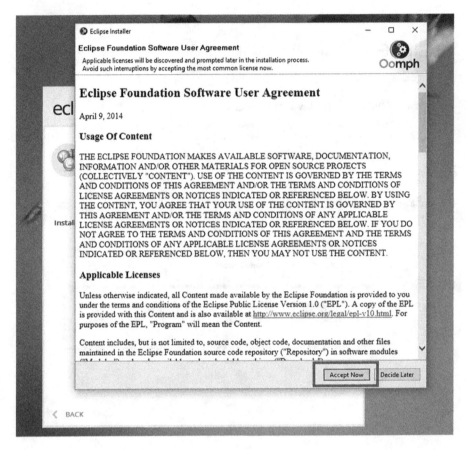

***Figure 4-9.*** *Accept the user agreement*

After installation is complete, you are ready to launch the IDE (Figure 4-10).

*Figure 4-10.* *Launching the IDE*

## Setting Up Eclipse

When you click Launch you'll see that in the next step the IDE will start for the first time (Figure 4-11).

**Figure 4-11.** *Eclipse Neon starts*

The first time you launch it the program will ask for a *workspace*, where you will save your projects (Figure 4-12).

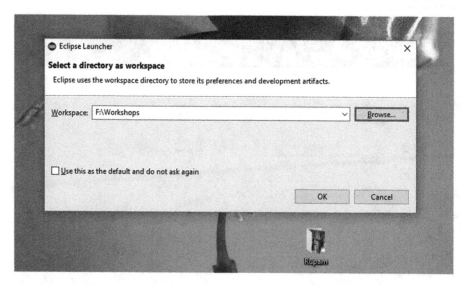

***Figure 4-12.*** *Selecting a workspace*

The IDE is opened and you are ready to start working with it (Figure 4-13).

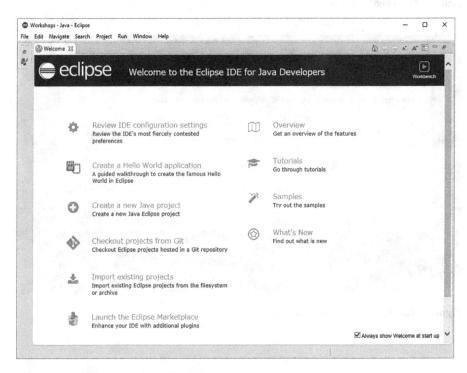

***Figure 4-13.*** *You have started the IDE*

To start a new project, click File ä New ä Java Project (Figure 4-14).

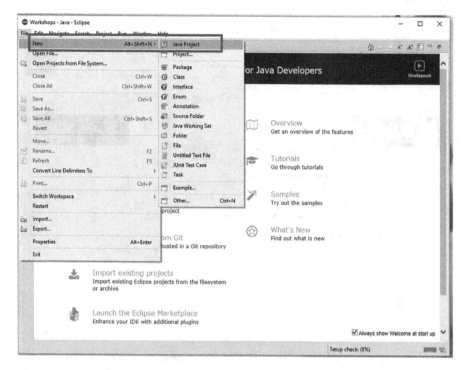

***Figure 4-14.*** *Starting a new project*

Give a name to the project such as "Example" and then select the JRE version and click Next (Figure 4-15).

**Figure 4-15.** *Name the project and then click Next*

Now you need to go to the Libraries tab, where you can add external JAR files (Figure 4-16).

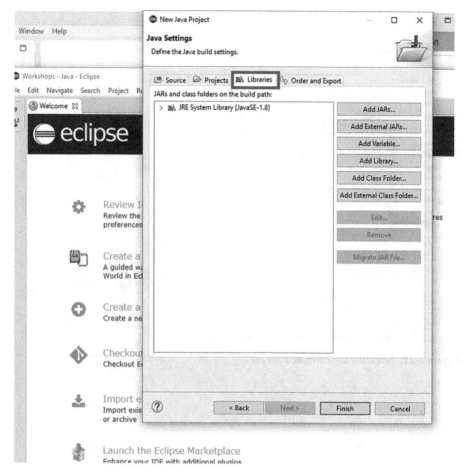

**Figure 4-16.** *Selecting the libraries option*

You can now add external JAR files from this tab. Select the LeapJava.jar file from the Leap SDK (Figure 4-17).

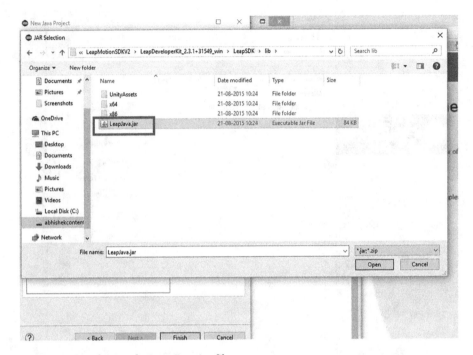

***Figure 4-17.*** *Selecting the LeapJava.jar file*

Looking at the content of the LeapJava.jar file, the most important part is the native library location (Figure 4-18). On the next screen you will see why the native library location is important.

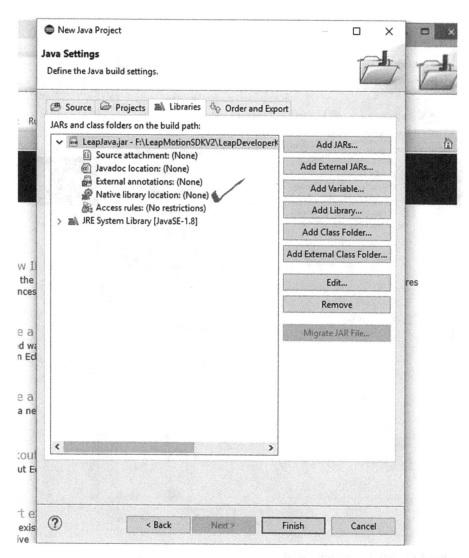

***Figure 4-18.*** *Checking the content of jar file*

Now select the Native Library Location option and click Edit (Figure 4-19). We select this option because we need to target the build so the options are either x86 or x64. For this book we will be targeting x64 because the machine I am working on, like most current computers, is 64-bit.

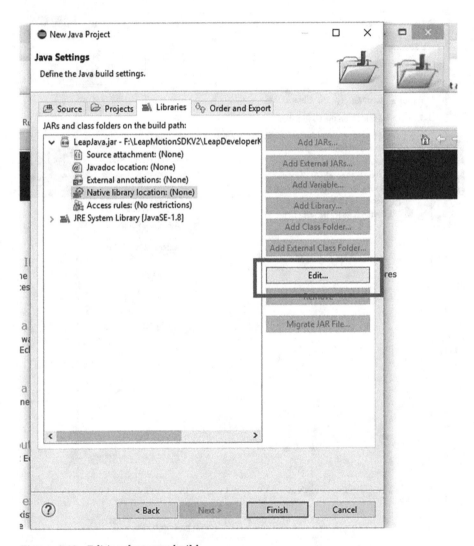

***Figure 4-19.*** *Editing the target build*

After choosing Edit you have the option to select the external folder for the target build (Figure 4-20).

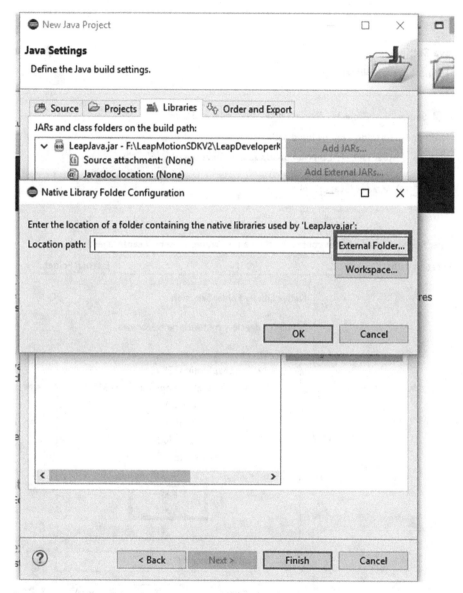

**Figure 4-20.** *Selecting an external folder*

Go to the library folder and select the target build as either x86 or x64 (Figure 4-21). This is an important step because it allows the program to run once it is compiled.

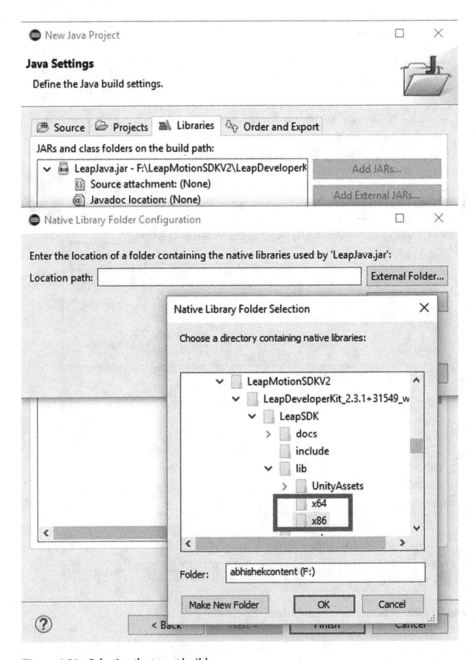

**Figure 4-21.** *Selecting the target build*

After selecting the build, click OK (Figure 4-22). You are ready to begin coding logic now.

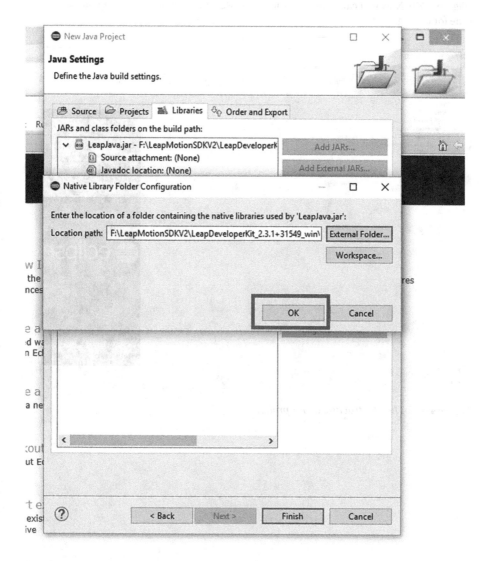

:h the Eclipse Marketplace

*Figure 4-22.* *Click OK to continue*

Now check the structure of the project created with the LeapMotion.jar file added (Figure 4-23). Now you can code easily for Leap Motion. Integration is complete; now it is time for coding.

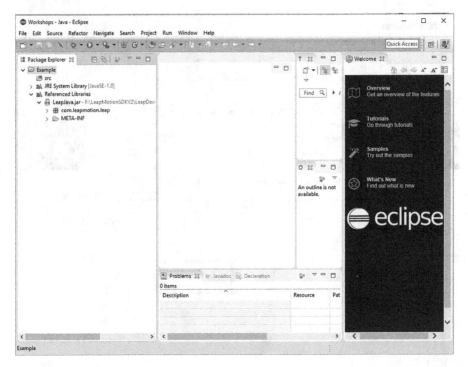

***Figure 4-23.*** *The file structure of our project*

# Let's Start Coding in Eclipse

In the previous section you set up the IDE for the Leap Motion sensor. In this section we will start with Java coding. I'll show you the basic steps to get the code up and running. The final code is shown in Listing 4-1 later in this section.

The first step is to create a class file where you will write the coding logic. The important thing here is adding the Leap Motion libraries to access important objects of the Leap Motion Controller.

Open your project, right-click the src folder, and then create a new class (Figure 4-24).

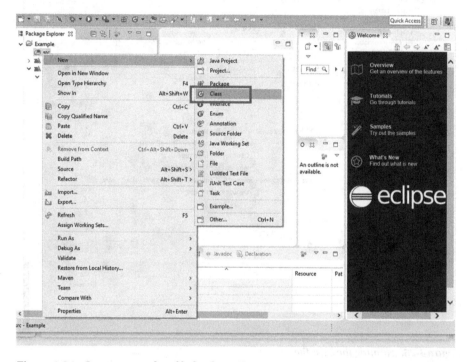

***Figure 4-24.*** *Create a new class file for the project*

In the next step, name the class file as LeapC and add a main method to it (Figure 4-25).

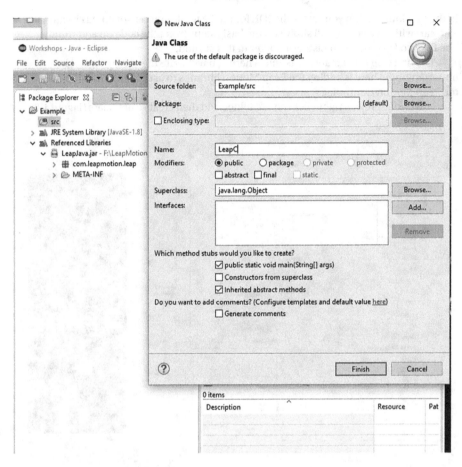

**Figure 4-25.** *Naming the class file*

The next step is to start importing the important libraries for use in the project. To launch the import option, type the following:

```
import com.leapmotion.leap.*;
```

This will add most of the libraries that are related to Leap Motion.

To capture gesture values, you need to add gesture capabilities through the library:

```
import java.io.IOException;
import com.leapmotion.leap.*;
import com.leapmotion.leap.Gesture.State;
```

In the next step you extend the Listener class (Figure 4-26). The keyword extends is used in Java for implementing inheritance (applying a property of a parent class to a subclass). In general terms, by using extends you are able to add features to an existing class.

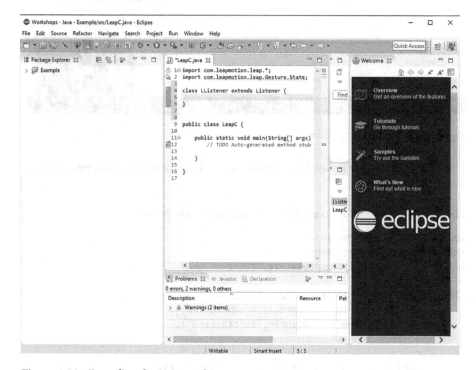

***Figure 4-26.*** *Extending the Listener class*

Now you can add the gesture logic (Figure 4-27).

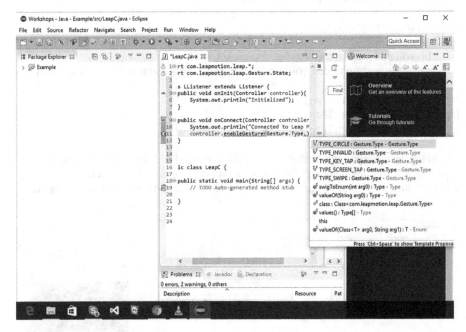

**Figure 4-27.** *Adding the gesture logic*

The complete code for reading gestures with the Leap Motion Controller is shown in Listing 4-1.

**Listing 4-1.** The Code for Accessing Gestures through Leap Motion

```java
import java.io.IOException;
import com.leapmotion.leap.*;
import com.leapmotion.leap.Gesture.State;

class LLListener extends Listener {
        public void onInit(Controller controller){
                System.out.println("Initialized");
        }

        public void onConnect(Controller controller){
                System.out.println("Connected to Leap Motion");
                controller.enableGesture(Gesture.Type.TYPE_CIRCLE);
                controller.enableGesture(Gesture.Type.TYPE_SWIPE);
                controller.enableGesture(Gesture.Type.TYPE_SCREEN_TAP);
                controller.enableGesture(Gesture.Type.TYPE_INVALID);
                controller.enableGesture(Gesture.Type.TYPE_KEY_TAP);
        }
```

```
        public void onDisconnect(Controller controller){
                System.out.println("Leap Motion is disconnected");
        }

        public void onExit(Controller controller){
                System.out.println("Exiting The app");
        }
}

public class LeapC {

        public static void main(String[] args) {
                // TODO Auto-generated method stub
                LListener listener =new LListener();
                Controller controller = new Controller();
                controller.addListener(listener);

                System.out.println("Press enter to quit");

                try {
                        System.in.read();
                }catch(IOException e){
                        e.printStackTrace();

                }
                controller.removeListener(listener);

        }

}
```

The program starts with the Listener class being extended. Then the onConnect method checks for all the gestures available for Leap Motion.

If the Leap Motion sensor is disconnected we display a message about that using the onDisconnect method.

The onExit method is called when the app is exited or closed.

Make sure the Leap Motion Controller is attached and then run the program through Eclipse. The output is as follows:

```
Initialized
Press enter to quit
Connected to Leap Motion
Leap Motion is disconnected
Connected to Leap Motion
```

The lifecycle of the app is complete. The full lifecycle can be seen in Figure 4-28.

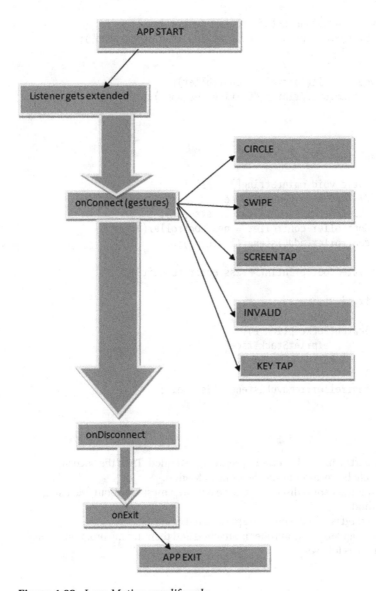

**Figure 4-28.** *Leap Motion app lifecycle*

# Summary

In this chapter we used the Eclipse IDE to get started with Leap Motion and Java. You saw the process of adding important libraries for using Leap Motion with Java. The chapter finished with a simple program that can be extended easily.

# CHAPTER 5

# Getting Started with Unity and Leap Motion

The previous chapter covered Java support for Leap Motion. In this chapter we will show how to integrate Leap Motion with the Unity game engine. We will first look at Unity's basic features and then start working with Leap Motion and Google Cardboard.

## The Unity Game Engine

Unity is one of the most versatile game engines used in the industry today. It supports 21 platforms (https://unity3d.com/).

The flow of control for Unity with some common platforms is shown in Figure 5-1.

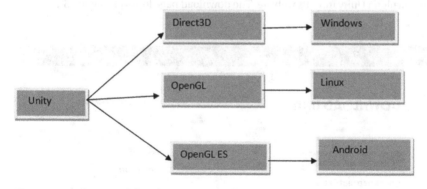

**Figure 5-1.** *The control flow for Unity*

As you can see, Unity uses Direct3D for Windows-based applications, OpenGL for Linux, and OpenGL ES for Android.

© Abhishek Nandy 2016

A. Nandy, *Leap Motion for Developers*, DOI 10.1007/978-1-4842-2550-9_5

Unity is rich in features; some of the most important ones are these:

- Lifelike animation
- Scripting with C#, JavaScript, or Boo
- Unmatched import pipeline
- Fully extensible editor
- State machines
- Blend trees
- Inverse kinematics
- Physics-based shading
- Shuriken-based particle system
- 2D physics
- Sprite packer
- Automatic sprite animation
- Multithreaded simulation
- Advanced vehicle physics

# Downloading Unity

You can download Unity from its website. The download page looks like Figure 5-2.

***Figure 5-2.*** *Downloading Unity*

Make sure that Unity is installed and you are set up. As the next step you need to download the core Unity assets for Leap Motion Orion (`https://developer.leapmotion.com/unity`), as shown in Figure 5-3).

***Figure 5-3.*** *Downloading Unity Leap Motion core assets*

# Getting Started with Unity

Let's start with a Unity project. First open Unity, name the new project, and keep the 3D toggle option on. Name the project LeapProject4 (Figure 5-4).

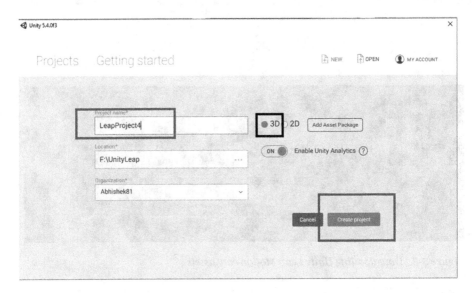

***Figure 5-4.*** *Creating a new project*

In the next step you will see the project window open; it will have blank content at this point (Figure 5-5).

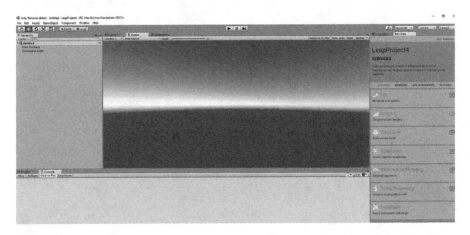

***Figure 5-5.*** *The project window is opened*

First you need to import, as a custom package (Figure 5-6), the Orion Unity package that you downloaded.

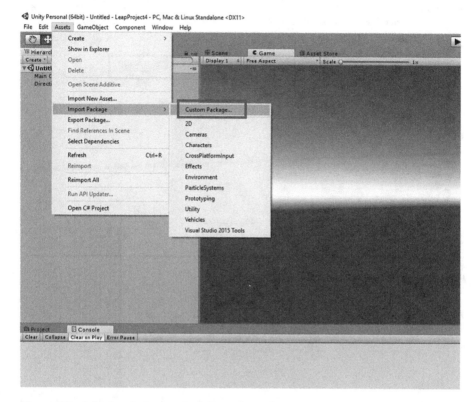

***Figure 5-6.*** *Selecting the Import Package option*

Make sure that you are copying the right package for installation (Figure 5-7).

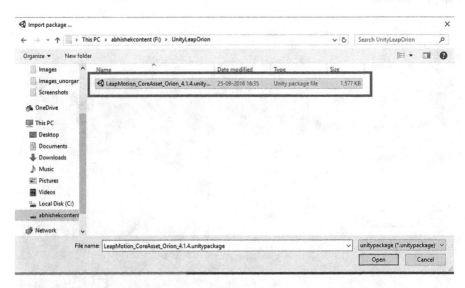

**Figure 5-7.** *The Leap Motion Orion package*

Now import every file of the package into the project and double-check that everything is copied (Figure 5-8).

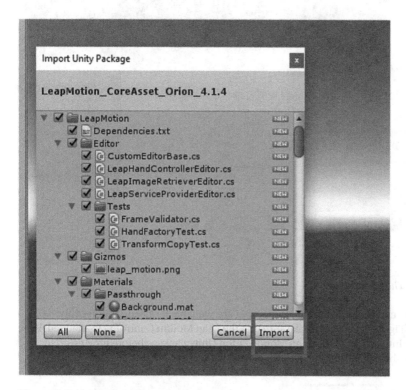

***Figure 5-8.*** *Importing the entire package*

When you copy the files you'll see that an entire file structure has been created (Figure 5-9). These files are to be used for our project purposes. The Scenes folder is the most important one.

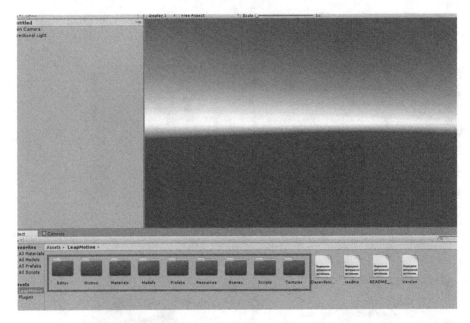

***Figure 5-9.*** *The file structure*

Now you can explore different scenes that are available for Leap Motion Unity integration (Figure 5-10). First make sure that the Leap Motion Controller is attached. We will start the integration of the Leap Motion Orion Unity package before moving on to demonstrate the Google platform for VR in the final section.

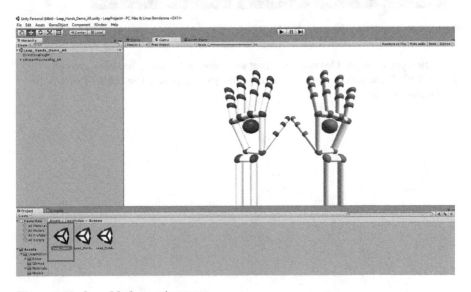

***Figure 5-10.*** *Leap Motion project scene*

You can now run the project. When you run the scene, you will see the output shown in Figure 5-11 via Leap Motion.

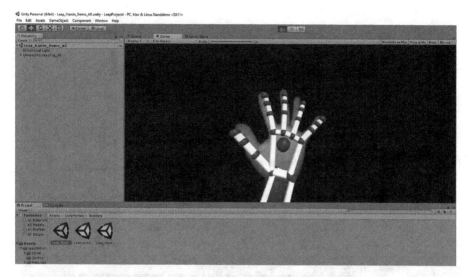

**Figure 5-11.** *The project running*

Now you can extend the project by downloading a package. Head to the asset store in Unity and search for Spiders. Download the free Fantasy Spider package as shown in Figure 5-12.

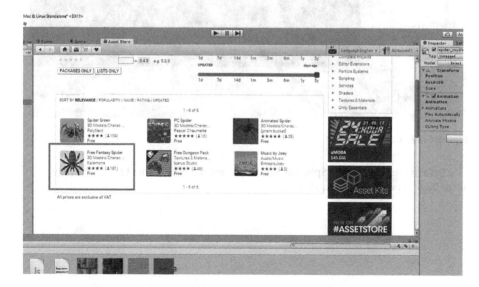

**Figure 5-12.** *Downloading a spider asset*

91

After importing the package, open the Fantasy Spider asset from the Assets folder in the same place where we are working with the project (Figure 5-13).

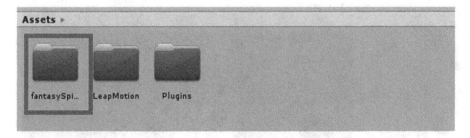

***Figure 5-13.*** *Opening the fantasySpider assets folder*

From the Leap Motion scenes folder open the Leap_Hands_Demo_AR scene and copy the LMheadmountedRig_AR object to the FantasySpider scene (Figure 5-14).

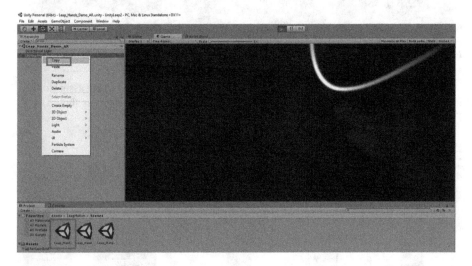

***Figure 5-14.*** *Copying the file*

Paste it into the Fantasy Spider scene and adjust the LMHeadmountedRig_AR view accordingly as shown in Figure 5-15.

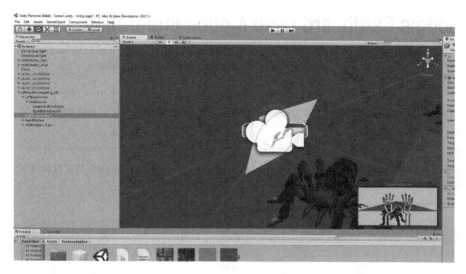

*Figure 5-15.* *Adjusting the view*

Run the application now to see the Leap Motion-controlled hands among the spiders (Figure 5-16).

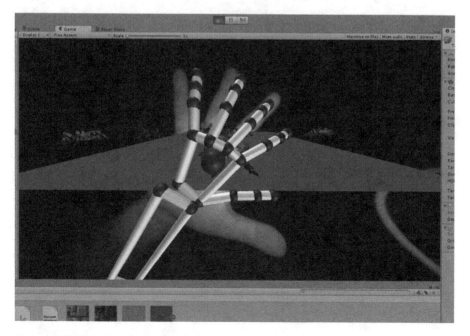

*Figure 5-16.* *Running the application*

# Google Cardboard Leap Motion Integration

In this section we will briefly show how to integrate the Google Cardboard SDK for Unity (`https://developers.google.com/vr/unity/download`) with Leap Motion.

---

■ **Note**    Google Cardboard is a simple and affordable VR system that is cheap and easy to set up.

---

First you need to download the Google Cardboard Unity SDK (Figure 5-17). This SDK will allow you to get started developing VR apps within Unity.

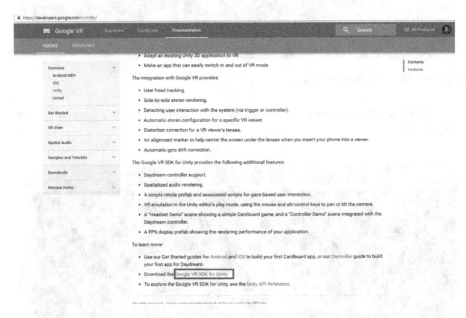

*Figure 5-17.   Google Cardboard VR*

Its project structure or control flow is shown in Figure 5-18.

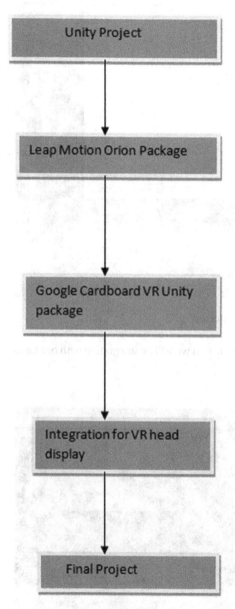

***Figure 5-18.*** *The complete Google Cardboard project structure*

Now you can start importing the Google VR package to Unity (Figure 5-19).

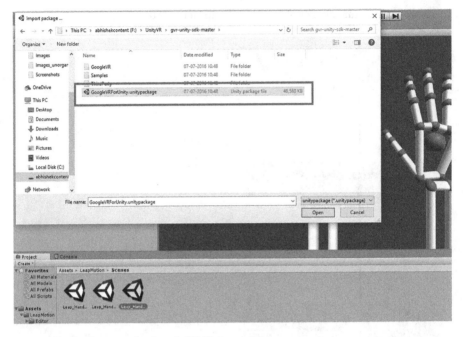

*Figure 5-19. Importing the Google VR Unity package*

Open the default head-mounted project file that we will be integrating with our Leap Motion scene (Figure 5-20).

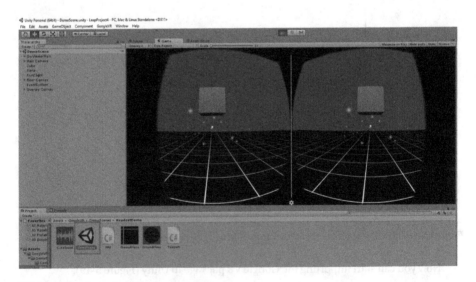

*Figure 5-20. Running the demo project*

To integrate Leap Motion with Google Cardboard you need to copy certain objects from the demo scene to the Leap Motion scene: GVR View Main, Event System, and Overlay Canvas, as shown in Figure 5-21.

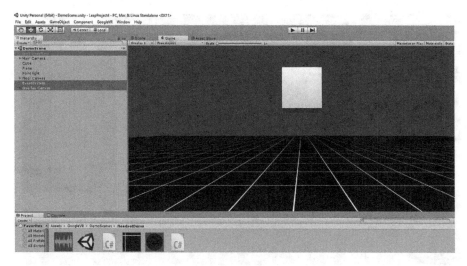

**Figure 5-21.** *Copying the objects from the demo scene*

With the objects pasted in, the Leap Motion scene now looks like Figure 5-22. Save the scene.

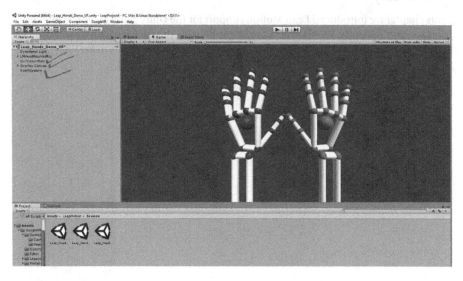

**Figure 5-22.** *The scene after copying all the objects*

Finally, run the saved project to see what it looks like in the head-mounted display (Figure 5-23).

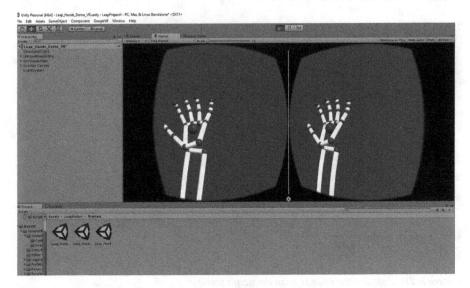

***Figure 5-23.*** *The scene runs with the Google Cardboard VR package*

# Summary

In this chapter we introduced Leap Motion support for the Unity game engine, using the Orion package for Unity. We showed an example of using the package with Unity and then extended Leap Motion support with the Google Cardboard platform for VR.

**CHAPTER 6**

■ ■ ■

# Leap Motion with Processing

In the previous chapter we discussed the integration of the Unity game platform with Leap Motion. In this chapter we will briefly introduce the Processing language and then integrate the Processing library for Leap Motion to create a sample application.

## Introducing Processing

Processing is a programming language specifically meant for *creative coding*. The most important part of Processing as a language is that it brings visual arts to life with the help of coding. It helps us to learn the fundamentals of computer programming by getting to see results visually.

It is an open source language and can run in multiple platforms. You can easily get going inside a Processing environment in the Windows, Linux, or MAC platforms. Processing is an IDE in which we program and the output is a visual interpretation of the code we write. The basic unit in which we code in Processing is considered a *sketch*. The extension of a file saved in Processing is .pde.

The inspiration for developing the Processing language came initially from OpenGL. It quickly developed an active community, and Processing has been extended to support multiple programming languages (Figure 6-1).

© Abhishek Nandy 2016
A. Nandy, *Leap Motion for Developers*, DOI 10.1007/978-1-4842-2550-9_6

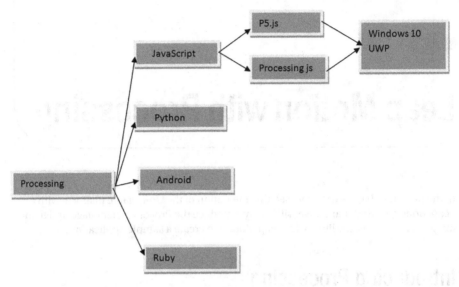

*Figure 6-1.* *The extension of Processing support*

## Environment

In this section I'll show you how to get ready for Processing.

## Setting Up the Environment in Windows

Processing is completely free and open source, and you can download it from the following link:

https://processing.org/download/?processing

For this book download the Windows version; Processing also supports both Mac and Linux.

## Configuration

As you download the file it comes in a Zip version, and you need to extract it. I used Winrar for extraction.

As you extract the zip file a folder is created, as shown in Figure 6-2.

processing-3.1.1

**Figure 6-2.** *The Processing folder*

Open the folder, where you'll get an executable link for running Processing (Figure 6-3).

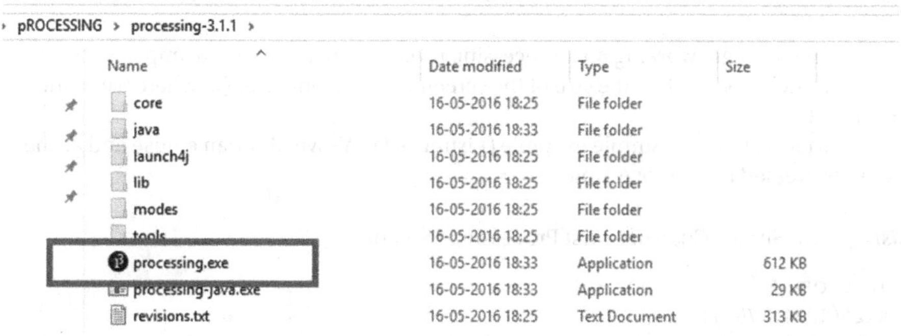

| › pROCESSING › processing-3.1.1 › | | | |
|---|---|---|---|
| Name | Date modified | Type | Size |
| core | 16-05-2016 18:25 | File folder | |
| java | 16-05-2016 18:33 | File folder | |
| launch4j | 16-05-2016 18:25 | File folder | |
| lib | 16-05-2016 18:25 | File folder | |
| modes | 16-05-2016 18:25 | File folder | |
| tools | 16-05-2016 18:25 | File folder | |
| processing.exe | 16-05-2016 18:33 | Application | 612 KB |
| processing-java.exe | 16-05-2016 18:33 | Application | 29 KB |
| revisions.txt | 16-05-2016 18:25 | Text Document | 313 KB |

**Figure 6-3.** *The executable for Processing*

# A First Processing App

The structure of a Processing app looks like Figure 6-4.

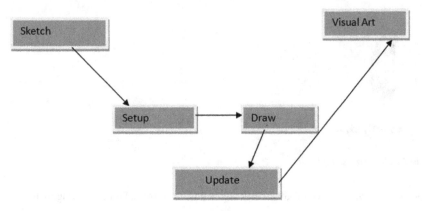

***Figure 6-4.*** *The structure of a Processing app*

When you begin working on a Processing project, two functions are important: setup(), where you declare the size of the screen window, and draw(), where we render the output.

Let's take a look at a simple example (Listing 6-1). We will draw an ellipse and as the mouse is pressed it will move around.

***Listing 6-1.*** Simple Code of a First Processing Example

```
void setup() {
  size(1024, 768);
  noSmooth();
  fill(126);
  background(102);
}

void draw() {
  if (mousePressed) {
    stroke(255);
  } else {
    stroke(0);
  }
  ellipse(mouseX-30, mouseY, mouseX+30, mouseY);
  ellipse(mouseX, mouseY-30, mouseX, mouseY+30);
}
```

Click on Run in the IDE to view the output (Figure 6-5).

***Figure 6-5.*** *Running the program in the IDE*

The output looks like Figure 6-6.

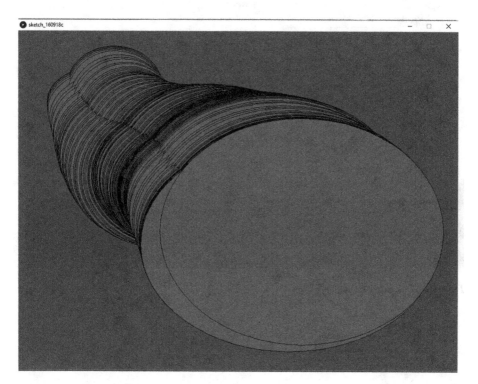

***Figure 6-6.*** *The output*

## Libraries

The other important aspect of Processing is its available support. There are more than 100 additional libraries for our usage with Processing. Let's take a glimpse at some important library options in Processing.

From the IDE go to Sketch ➤ Import Library ➤ Add Library as shown in Figure 6-7.

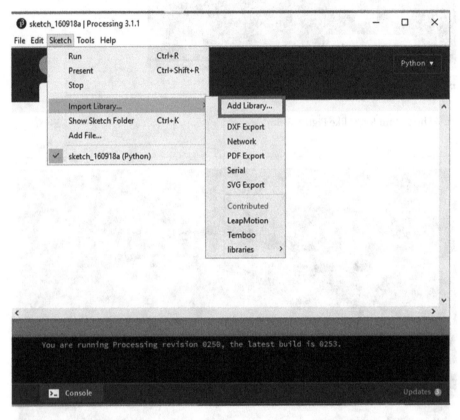

*Figure 6-7. Adding libraries*

The library options available from the Processing IDE are listed, as shown in Figure 6-8.

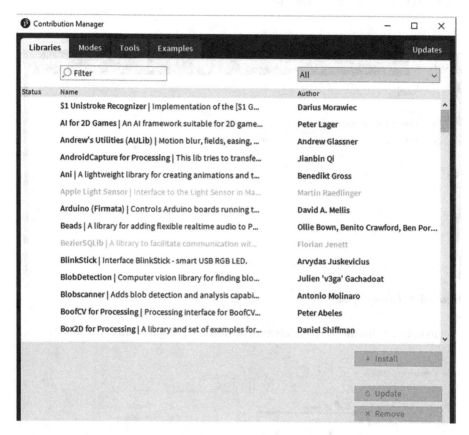

*Figure 6-8. Library options in Processing*

The library that we need to search for will include the "Leap" keyword. This will verify that the Leap Motion Library is installed. If is the Status column shows a green tick mark, we know it is installed (Figure 6-9).

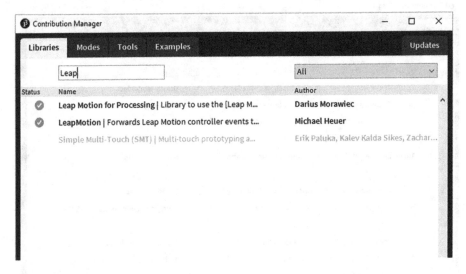

***Figure 6-9.*** *Library options*

You can see that there are two libraries in Processing (Figure 6-10).

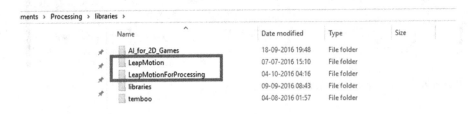

***Figure 6-10.*** *Two Leap Motion libraries*

After adding the libraries, the next step is to add references to them. We will be giving examples for both of them.

# Leap Motion Processing Integration

Figure 6-11 shows the process of integrating Processing with Leap Motion.

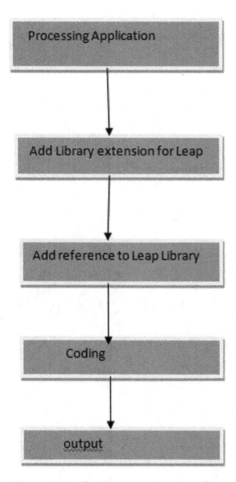

***Figure 6-11.*** *The Processing Leap App flow*

To try out this sequence, let's check an example. Make sure the Leap Motion Controller is attached.

The code of the program is shown in Listing 6-2.

***Listing 6-2.*** The Code for the Initial Processing Demo Program

```
import de.voidplus.leapmotion.*;

// ==========================================================
// Table of Contents:
// ├─ 1. Callbacks
// ├─ 2. Hand
// ├─ 3. Arms
// ├─ 4. Fingers
// ├─ 5. Bones
// ├─ 6. Tools
// └─ 7. Devices
// ==========================================================

LeapMotion leap;

void setup() {
  size(800, 500);
  background(255);
  // ...

  leap = new LeapMotion(this);
}

// ==========================================================
// 1. Callbacks

void leapOnInit() {
  // println("Leap Motion Init");
}
void leapOnConnect() {
  // println("Leap Motion Connect");
}
void leapOnFrame() {
  // println("Leap Motion Frame");
}
void leapOnDisconnect() {
  // println("Leap Motion Disconnect");
}
void leapOnExit() {
  // println("Leap Motion Exit");
}
```

```
void draw() {
  background(255);
  // ...

  int fps = leap.getFrameRate();
  for (Hand hand : leap.getHands ()) {

    // =====================================================
    // 2. Hand

    int     handId              = hand.getId();
    PVector handPosition        = hand.getPosition();
    PVector handStabilized      = hand.getStabilizedPosition();
    PVector handDirection       = hand.getDirection();
    PVector handDynamics        = hand.getDynamics();
    float   handRoll            = hand.getRoll();
    float   handPitch           = hand.getPitch();
    float   handYaw             = hand.getYaw();
    boolean handIsLeft          = hand.isLeft();
    boolean handIsRight         = hand.isRight();
    float   handGrab            = hand.getGrabStrength();
    float   handPinch           = hand.getPinchStrength();
    float   handTime            = hand.getTimeVisible();
    PVector spherePosition      = hand.getSpherePosition();
    float   sphereRadius        = hand.getSphereRadius();

    // ----------------------------------------------------
    // Drawing
    hand.draw();

    // =====================================================
    // 3. Arm

    if (hand.hasArm()) {
      Arm     arm               = hand.getArm();
      float   armWidth          = arm.getWidth();
      PVector armWristPos        = arm.getWristPosition();
      PVector armElbowPos        = arm.getElbowPosition();
    }

    // =====================================================
    // 4. Finger

    Finger  fingerThumb         = hand.getThumb();
    // or                         hand.getFinger("thumb");
    // or                         hand.getFinger(0);
```

109

```
Finger   fingerIndex       = hand.getIndexFinger();
// or                        hand.getFinger("index");
// or                        hand.getFinger(1);

Finger   fingerMiddle      = hand.getMiddleFinger();
// or                        hand.getFinger("middle");
// or                        hand.getFinger(2);
Finger   fingerRing        = hand.getRingFinger();
// or                        hand.getFinger("ring");
// or                        hand.getFinger(3);

Finger   fingerPink        = hand.getPinkyFinger();
// or                        hand.getFinger("pinky");
// or                        hand.getFinger(4);

for (Finger finger : hand.getFingers()) {
  // or               hand.getOutstretchedFingers();
  // or               hand.getOutstretchedFingersByAngle();

  int     fingerId         = finger.getId();
  PVector fingerPosition   = finger.getPosition();
  PVector fingerStabilized = finger.getStabilizedPosition();
  PVector fingerVelocity   = finger.getVelocity();
  PVector fingerDirection  = finger.getDirection();
  float   fingerTime       = finger.getTimeVisible();
  // ----------------------------------------------
  // Drawing

  // Drawing:
  // finger.draw();  // Executes drawBones() and drawJoints()
  // finger.drawBones();
  // finger.drawJoints();

  // -----------------------------------------------
  // Selection

  switch(finger.getType()) {
  case 0:
    // System.out.println("thumb");
    break;
  case 1:
    // System.out.println("index");
    break;
  case 2:
    // System.out.println("middle");
    break;
```

```
      case 3:
        // System.out.println("ring");
        break;
      case 4:
        // System.out.println("pinky");
        break;
    }


    // ================================================
    // 5. Bones
    // --------
    // https://developer.leapmotion.com/documentation/java/devguide/Leap_
Overview.html#Layer_1

      Bone    boneDistal       = finger.getDistalBone();
      // or                      finger.get("distal");
      // or                      finger.getBone(0);

      Bone    boneIntermediate = finger.getIntermediateBone();
      // or                      finger.get("intermediate");
      // or                      finger.getBone(1);
      Bone    boneProximal     = finger.getProximalBone();
      // or                      finger.get("proximal");
      // or                      finger.getBone(2);

      Bone    boneMetacarpal   = finger.getMetacarpalBone();
      // or                      finger.get("metacarpal");
      // or                      finger.getBone(3);

    // ----------------------------------------------------
    // Touch emulation

      int     touchZone        = finger.getTouchZone();
      float   touchDistance    = finger.getTouchDistance();

    switch(touchZone) {
    case -1: // None
      break;
    case 0: // Hovering
      // println("Hovering (#" + fingerId + "): " + touchDistance);
      break;
    case 1: // Touching
      // println("Touching (#" + fingerId + ")");
      break;
    }
  }
```

111

```
// ========================================================
// 6. Tools

for (Tool tool : hand.getTools()) {
  int     toolId          = tool.getId();
  PVector toolPosition    = tool.getPosition();
  PVector toolStabilized  = tool.getStabilizedPosition();
  PVector toolVelocity    = tool.getVelocity();
  PVector toolDirection   = tool.getDirection();
  float   toolTime        = tool.getTimeVisible();


  // ------------------------------------------------
  // Drawing:
  // tool.draw();


  // ------------------------------------------------
  // Touch emulation

  int     touchZone       = tool.getTouchZone();
  float   touchDistance   = tool.getTouchDistance();

  switch(touchZone) {
  case -1: // None
    break;
  case 0: // Hovering
    // println("Hovering (#" + toolId + "): " + touchDistance);
    break;
  case 1: // Touching
    // println("Touching (#" + toolId + ")");
    break;
  }
 }
}


// ========================================================
// 7. Devices

for (Device device : leap.getDevices()) {
  float deviceHorizontalViewAngle = device.getHorizontalViewAngle();
  float deviceVericalViewAngle = device.getVerticalViewAngle();
  float deviceRange = device.getRange();
 }
}
```

When we run the program, it first shows the bones, arm points, and so on it needs to run interactively (Figure 6-12).

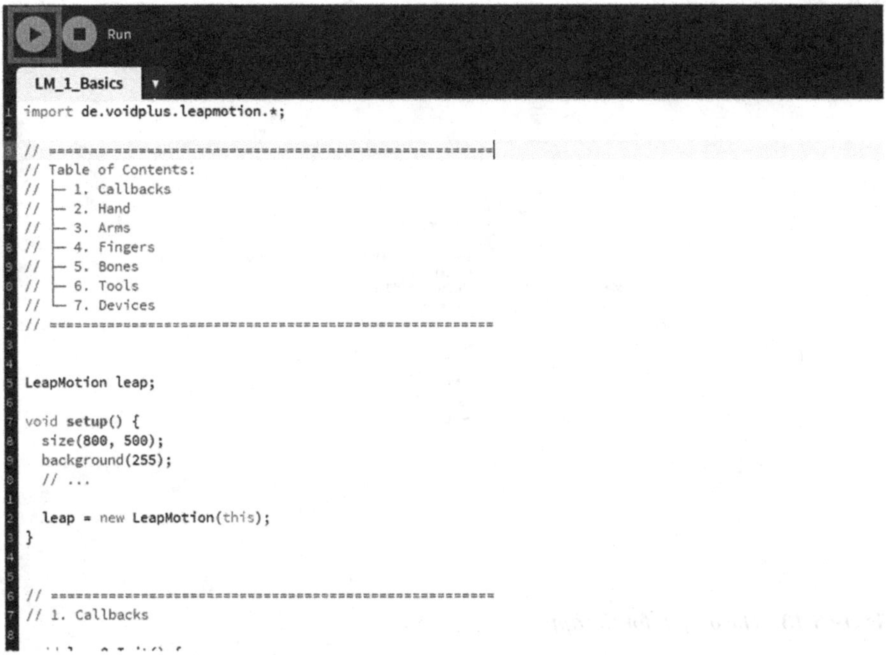

```
import de.voidplus.leapmotion.*;

// ========================================================
// Table of Contents:
// ├─ 1. Callbacks
// ├─ 2. Hand
// ├─ 3. Arms
// ├─ 4. Fingers
// ├─ 5. Bones
// ├─ 6. Tools
// └─ 7. Devices
// ========================================================


LeapMotion leap;

void setup() {
  size(800, 500);
  background(255);
  // ...

  leap = new LeapMotion(this);
}


// ========================================================
// 1. Callbacks
```

*Figure 6-12. Running the program*

As we run the program, its output will be rendered as shown in Figure 6-13.

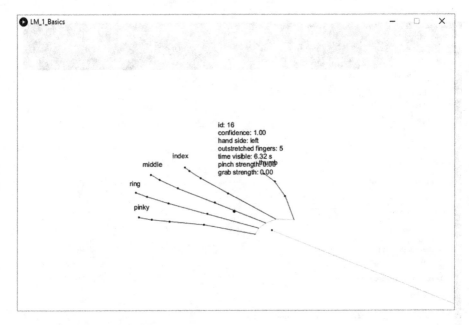

**Figure 6-13.** *The output for the app*

# Exporting the Application

Now you can save the application (Figure 6-14) and see how to export it for different operating systems.

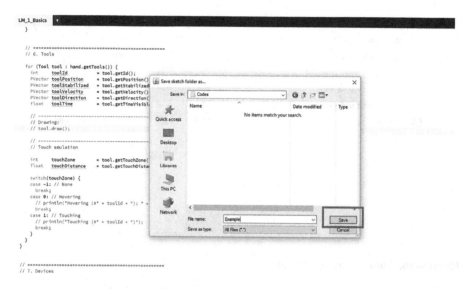

**Figure 6-14.** *Saving the file*

After saving the file, to export it you need to use the Export option from the Processing IDE. So from the Processing IDE, click File ➤ Export. When you click Export we will see the options for exporting to both Windows and Linux. Check both Windows and Linux as shown in Figure 6-15.

**Figure 6-15.** *We will export the application to both Windows and Linux*

After you export the application, you'll see that folders for Linux and Windows have been created, as shown in Figure 6-16.

| orïemplate > LeapMotion > Chaptero > Codes > Example | | ✓ ↻ Search Example | |
|---|---|---|---|
| Name ^ | Date modified | Type | Size |
| application.linux32 | 04-10-2016 17:14 | File folder | |
| application.linux64 | 04-10-2016 17:14 | File folder | |
| application.linux-armv6hf | 04-10-2016 17:14 | File folder | |
| application.windows32 | 04-10-2016 17:14 | File folder | |
| application.windows64 | 04-10-2016 17:14 | File folder | |
| Example.pde | 04-10-2016 17:09 | Processing Source... | |

***Figure 6-16.*** *The exported application*

Now double-click application.windows64 to verify that the application runs correctly after being exported. You will see an exe file called Example.exe (Figure 6-17); double-click to execute it.

| AuthorTemplate > LeapMotion > Chapter6 > Chapter6_Codes > Example > application.windows64 > | | | |
|---|---|---|---|
| Name ^ | Date modified | Type | Size |
| lib | 04-10-2016 17:14 | File folder | |
| source | 04-10-2016 17:14 | File folder | |
| Example.exe | 04-10-2016 17:14 | Application | 86 KB |

***Figure 6-17.*** *The exported application*

When the application is run as an exe, the output is as shown in Figure 6-18.

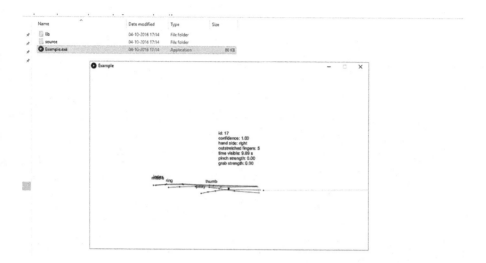

*Figure 6-18.* *Running the exe*

# Summary

In this chapter we have introduced the Processing language and integrated it with Leap Motion. We exported a sample app to different operating systems.

■ ■ ■

# CHAPTER 7

# Leap Motion with Unreal Engine 4

In the previous chapter you saw how Leap Motion is integrated with the Processing language IDE; in this chapter we will start with the game development platform Unreal Engine 4.13. We will first show how to download the latest version of Unreal Engine 4 and get started with it. Then we'll explore integrating the Leap Motion Controller with it and finally try some project examples integrating Leap Motion with Unreal Engine 4.

## Unreal Engine 4.13

In this section we will start by acquiring Unreal 4 and show the steps to installing it. To download Unreal Engine 4, go to https://www.unrealengine.com/what-is-unreal-engine-4 and click Get Unreal (Figure 7-1).

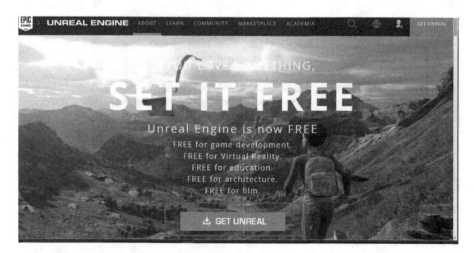

*Figure 7-1.* *The download link for Unreal Engine 4*

© Abhishek Nandy 2016
A. Nandy, *Leap Motion for Developers*, DOI 10.1007/978-1-4842-2550-9_7

We will be working with the latest version of Unreal Engine 4 (v.4.13 as of now) to get started with Leap Motion and Unreal Engine 4.

You will need to use credentials for downloading the Unreal 4 Engine. If you don't have an account with Epic Games you will need to create one. After entering your credentials, click Sign In (Figure 7-2).

*Figure 7-2. Logging in to start the download*

Accept the agreement to continue (Figure 7-3).

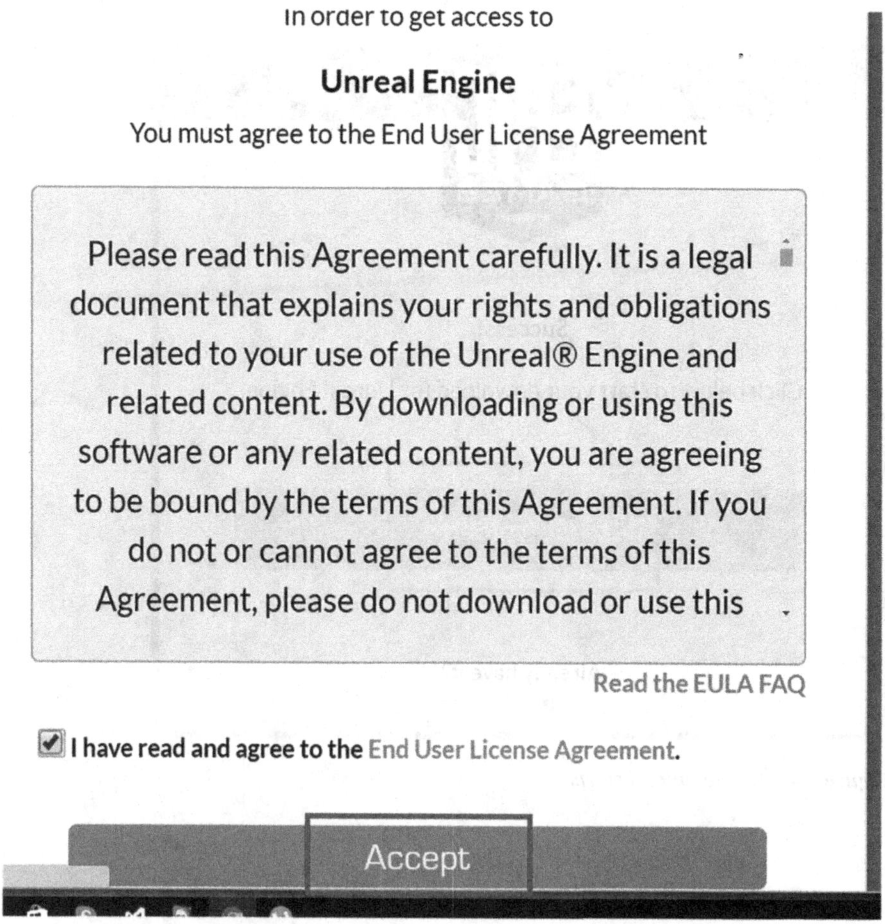

In order to get access to

## Unreal Engine

You must agree to the End User License Agreement

Please read this Agreement carefully. It is a legal
document that explains your rights and obligations
related to your use of the Unreal® Engine and
related content. By downloading or using this
software or any related content, you are agreeing
to be bound by the terms of this Agreement. If you
do not or cannot agree to the terms of this
Agreement, please do not download or use this

Read the EULA FAQ

☑ I have read and agree to the End User License Agreement.

Accept

*Figure 7-3. Accept the EULA*

In the next step, after accepting the EULA, you will be instructed to go ahead with installation. Click Download (Figure 7-4).

*Figure 7-4.* *The download starts*

In the next step you will see that the launcher has begun installing, and it will ask for a location. Click OK to continue (Figure 7-5).

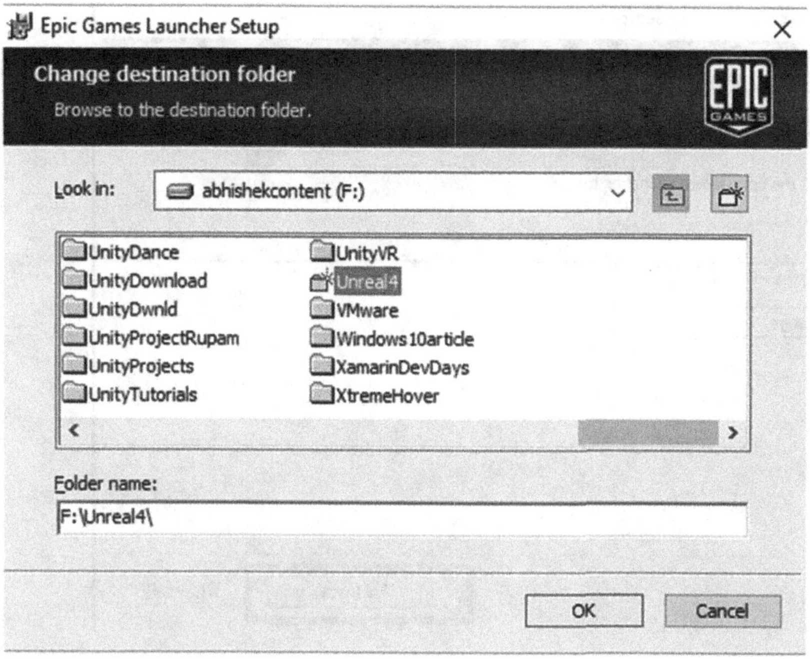

*Figure 7-5.* *The download starts*

On the next screen, confirm the destination and then click the Install button (Figure 7-6).

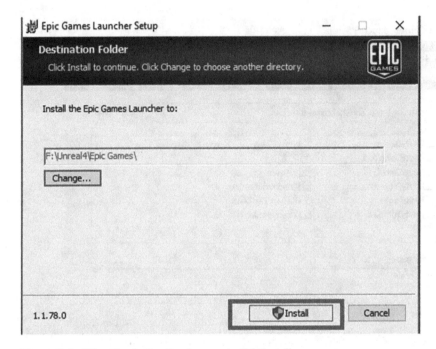

Figure 7-6. *When the destination is correct, click Install*

The installer will show you its progress (Figure 7-7).

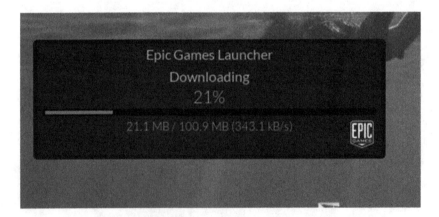

Figure 7-7. *The Epic Games Launcher is being installed*

In the next step, prerequisites are installed (Figure 7-8).

*Figure 7-8.* *prerequistes being installed*

The Epic Games Launcher will open up (Figure 7-9).

*Figure 7-9.* *The Epic Games Launcher*

In the next step you have the option to install the Unreal 4 Game Engine version (Figure 7-10). I have installed the latest one released at this time, 4.13.

***Figure 7-10.*** *The installation option for Unreal Engine 4*

The final step allows us to start modifying the installation with any necessary steps (Figure 7-11).

***Figure 7-11.*** *Unreal Engine 4.13 initializes*

# Creating a Project

After initialization you are ready start creating a new project. Follow these steps to integrate Leap motion with Unreal Engine 4:

1. Create a new project.

2. Open the project.

3. Enable the Leap Motion plugin.

4. Add a Blueprint class.

5. Then add a Game mode.

6. Finally, add the Leap Motion option.

With respect to an example the steps workflow is as shown in Figure 7-12.

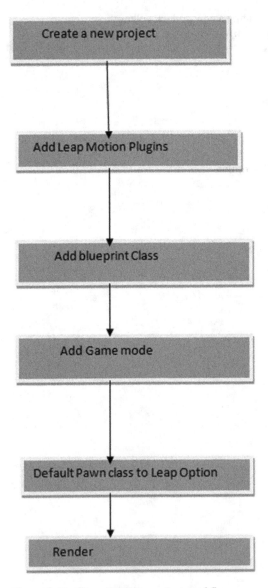

*Figure 7-12.* *Unreal Engine project workflow*

Let's see an example.

Start by creating a new project with blank content and the Blueprint option (Figure 7-13).

*Figure 7-13.* *Creating a new project*

You'll see that the project launches as specified (Figure 7-14).

*Figure 7-14.* *The new project launches*

Let's work on some examples.

# Starting a New Project

First create a new project (Figure 7-15).

***Figure 7-15.*** *Create a new project*

Take a blank project, name it LeapVariationHand, and click Create Project (Figure 7-16).

***Figure 7-16.** Naming the project*

When the project opens it looks like Figure 7-17.

***Figure 7-17.** The project opens*

The next step is to search for the Leap Motion plugin, which is available in Edit ➤ Plugins (Figure 7-18).

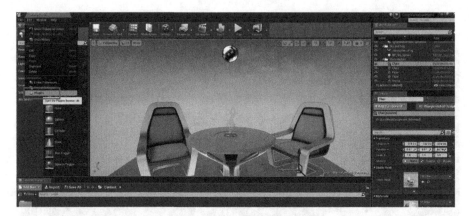

***Figure 7-18.*** *The project at first instance*

You also need to enable the Leap Motion plugin from the Input Devices option of the Plugins tab (Figure 7-19).

***Figure 7-19.*** *Enabling the plugin*

After you've enabled the plugin, Unreal Engine 4 requires a restart. Click Restart Now (Figure 7-20).

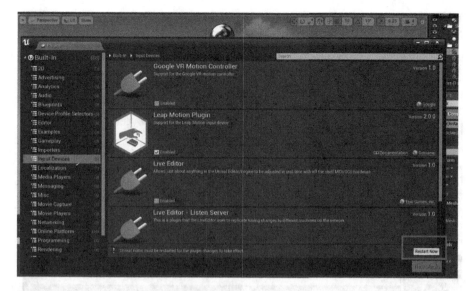

**Figure 7-20.** *Restarting Unreal Engine 4*

In order to keep the scene empty, you will delete the chair object as well as the table (Figure 7-21) so that you can see a clean view of the Leap Motion hand that we are using for recognition.

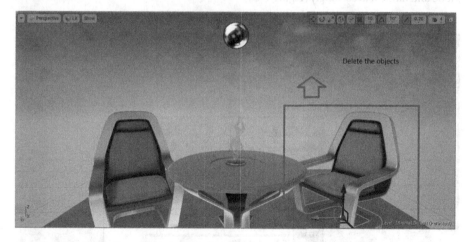

**Figure 7-21.** *Removing objects to keep the scene empty*

In the next step you can see that the scene is empty and it's time to create a Blueprint class (Figure 7-22).

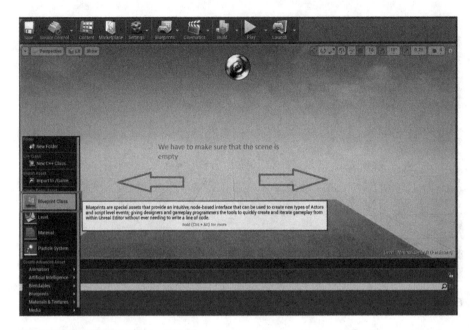

***Figure 7-22.*** *Adding a Blueprint class*

After adding a Blueprint class, you have an option to add a parent class; select Game Mode and name it accordingly (Figure 7-23).

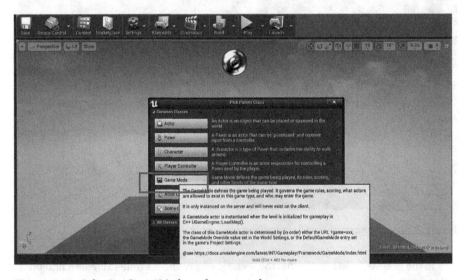

***Figure 7-23.*** *Selecting Game Mode as the parent class*

Name the game mode LeapEx. After its creation you will see a game controller icon, as in Figure 7-24. The Game Mode option is the way the game is to be played, so we will have to implement Leap Motion logic here.

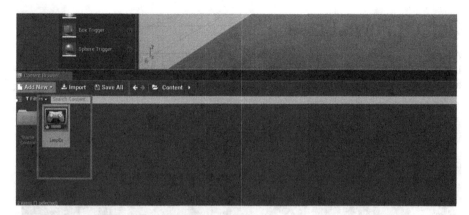

*Figure 7-24. Game mode name*

Now for the project settings, select Maps & Modes ➤ Default Modes and change the default game mode to the game mode name we have chosen (Figure 7-25). The name is LeapEx.

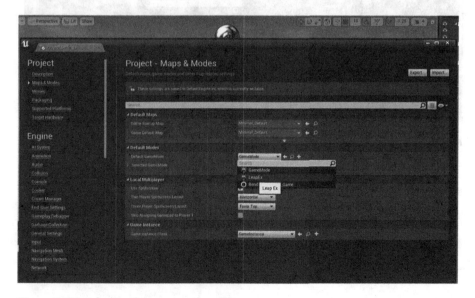

*Figure 7-25. Selecting the game mode option*

Now on the Selected Game Mode option you'll find lots of rigged avatars of hands that you can use for our interaction with the Leap Motion sensor. As an example we will cover the Default Pawn Class options for the Leap Motion sensor.

# Default Pawn Class

A pawn class is a base class of all actors in Unreal Engine4 that can be controlled by the AI implementation as done by the characters in the game scene. A pawn component can be added to different movement bindings. Choose the Leap binding as shown in Figure 7-26.

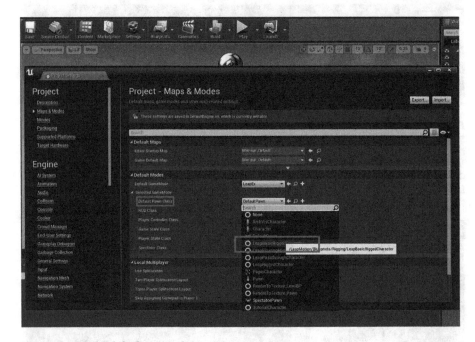

**Figure 7-26.** *The default pawn class option*

You can now run the modified game from the Play option in standalone mode. The game starts (Figure 7-27).

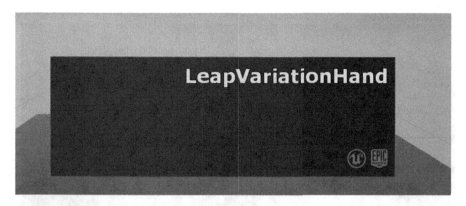

**Figure 7-27.** *The game starts running*

The game as it runs with interaction from the Leap Motion sensor is shown in Figure 7-28.

**Figure 7-28.** *The game running in play mode with a rigged Leap Motion hand*

Another variation of the pawn class with different settings that we can try is rigged mapping. This option allows a camera view for the Leap Motion sensor, so when we enable it we will see the functionality as shown in Figure 7-29. It captures the area the Leap Motion Controller can cover.

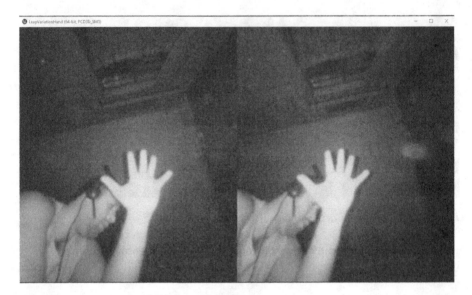

**Figure 7-29.** *Another variation of the pawn class*

# Summary

In this chapter we first downloaded and introduced Unreal Engine 4. Then we tried a project and went on to integrate the Leap Motion sensor to it. We also worked with different examples of using the Leap Motion Controller with Unreal 4.

# CHAPTER 8

## More on Unreal Engine 4 and Leap Motion

In the previous chapter we showed how to integrate Leap Motion with Unreal Engine 4. In this chapter we will extend it further.

## Extending the Project

Copy the plugin content to the main project we are working on (Figure 8-1).

*Figure 8-1.* *Naming the content*

© Abhishek Nandy 2016

139

A. Nandy, *Leap Motion for Developers*, DOI 10.1007/978-1-4842-2550-9_8

Now open up the plugin content, and you will see there is already a predefined blueprint (Figure 8-2).

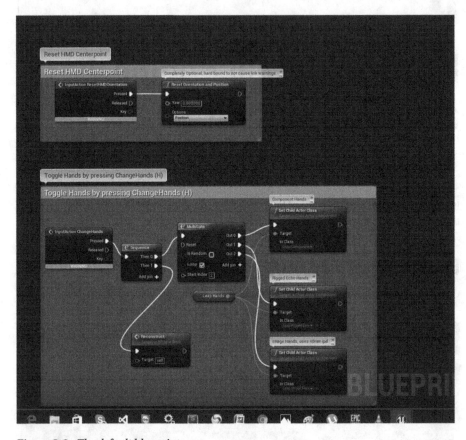

***Figure 8-2.*** *The default blueprint*

Within Project Settings, go to Engine ➤ Input ➤ Action Mappings and name the blueprint Change_hands (Figure 8-3).

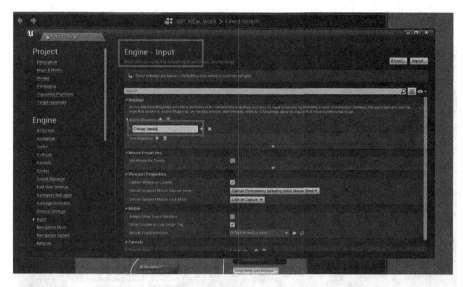

**Figure 8-3.** *Changing hand binding*

The way the logic of this blueprint works, whenever we press the H key on the keyboard we'll see a different hand (Figure 8-4).

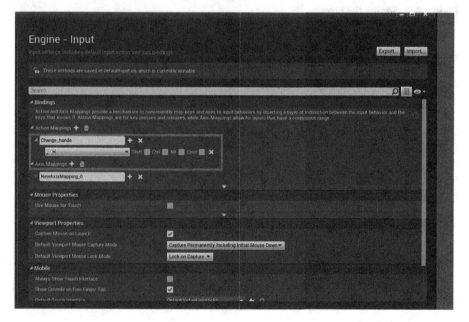

**Figure 8-4.** *Changing engine input*

You now need to save the project (Figure 8-5).

*Figure 8-5.* *Saving the project*

The blueprint to toggle hands with h looks as shown in Figure 8-6.

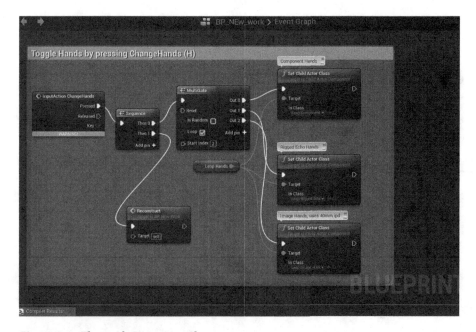

**Figure 8-6.** *The toggle H event graph*

The output looks like as shown in Figure 8-7. While toggling with H the hand appearance changes for Leap Motion interaction.

**Figure 8-7.** *The hand changes with toggle H keystroke*

Another toggle with H results in Figure 8-8.

*Figure 8-8.* *Variance with the hand mapping*

# Summary

We have extended Unreal Engine 4 further with an example here to give more options for integrating the game engine with Leap Motion.

# CHAPTER 9

■ ■ ■

# Setting Up Leap Motion with JavaScript

In this chapter we will start with the integration of Leap Motion with JavaScript and also see how the ThreeJS library is useful. Finally, we'll implement a Leap cursor with the Windows 10 UWP app.

## JavaScript and Leap Motion Sensor

HTML5 and JavaScript are the best combination for working with the web. So if we want to integrate the Leap Motion Controller with web applications, JavaScript is the obvious choice. The easy way to write coding logic with JavaScript and Leap Motion is to include the JavaScript library within an HTML5 page and implement the logic you need to apply for Leap Motion. The flow for this approach is shown in Figure 9-1.

© Abhishek Nandy 2016

A. Nandy, *Leap Motion for Developers*, DOI 10.1007/978-1-4842-2550-9_9

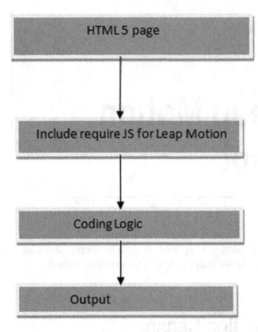

**Figure 9-1.** *The control flow for JavaScript with Leap Motion*

# CSS Visualizer

To build a JavaScript app, we will implement the logic outlined in the diagram. Let's take a look at a CSS visualizer.

A CSS visualizer is a visualization created by the LeapMotionJS framework using DOM elements and CSS3 animation and transforms. The LeapMotionJS framework is available for download at github (https://github.com/leapmotion/leapjs).

Download the entire code repository, as shown in Figure 9-2.

***Figure 9-2.*** *Downloading the repository*

When it is saved a zip file with the name `Leap-js-master.zip` will be available. Extract the file using any zip utility. All of the examples will be there in the examples folder (Figure 9-3).

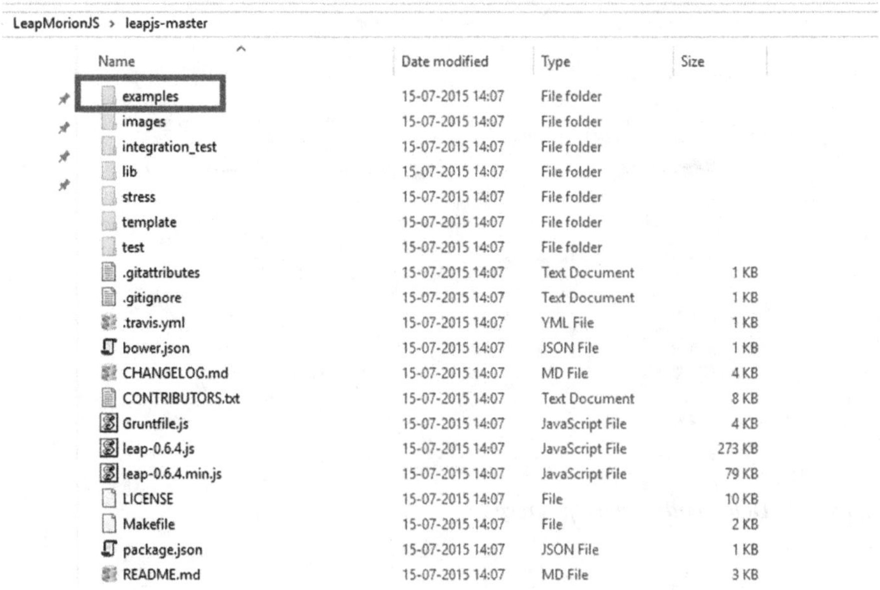

| Name | Date modified | Type | Size |
|---|---|---|---|
| examples | 15-07-2015 14:07 | File folder | |
| images | 15-07-2015 14:07 | File folder | |
| integration_test | 15-07-2015 14:07 | File folder | |
| lib | 15-07-2015 14:07 | File folder | |
| stress | 15-07-2015 14:07 | File folder | |
| template | 15-07-2015 14:07 | File folder | |
| test | 15-07-2015 14:07 | File folder | |
| .gitattributes | 15-07-2015 14:07 | Text Document | 1 KB |
| .gitignore | 15-07-2015 14:07 | Text Document | 1 KB |
| .travis.yml | 15-07-2015 14:07 | YML File | 1 KB |
| bower.json | 15-07-2015 14:07 | JSON File | 1 KB |
| CHANGELOG.md | 15-07-2015 14:07 | MD File | 4 KB |
| CONTRIBUTORS.txt | 15-07-2015 14:07 | Text Document | 8 KB |
| Gruntfile.js | 15-07-2015 14:07 | JavaScript File | 4 KB |
| leap-0.6.4.js | 15-07-2015 14:07 | JavaScript File | 273 KB |
| leap-0.6.4.min.js | 15-07-2015 14:07 | JavaScript File | 79 KB |
| LICENSE | 15-07-2015 14:07 | File | 10 KB |
| Makefile | 15-07-2015 14:07 | File | 2 KB |
| package.json | 15-07-2015 14:07 | JSON File | 1 KB |
| README.md | 15-07-2015 14:07 | MD File | 3 KB |

LeapMorionJS > leapjs-master

***Figure 9-3.*** *The Examples folder contains demos*

The code for the app is shown in Listing 9-1. We will use the LeapMotion JavaScript library, which works with the Leap Motion Controller.

Animations are made by styling using CSS3, with finger detection and hand module being made within the style tag. There are two functions, `movefinger` and `movesphere`, which identify finger and hand detection using the LeapJS framework.

We capture frame data using `Leap.loop;` within its content we capture both finger and hand data.

***Listing 9-1.*** The Leap Loop

```
Leap.loop(function (frame) {
//content
});
```

The other part of the code creates points for detecting finger and hand movements, all within the capability of CSS3 (Listing 9-2).

*Listing 9-2.* A CSS visualizer

```
<html>
  <head>
    <title>DOM Visualizer - Leap</title>
    <script src="../leap-0.6.4.js"></script>
    <script>
      function moveFinger(Finger, posX, posY, posZ) {
        Finger.style.webkitTransform = "translate3d("+posX+"px, "+posY+"px,
        "+posZ+"px)";
      }

      function moveSphere(Sphere, posX, posY, posZ, rotX, rotY, rotZ) {
        Sphere.style.webkitTransform = Sphere.style.mozTransform =
        Sphere.style.transform = "translateX("+posX+"px)
        translateY("+posY+"px) translateZ("+posZ+"px) rotateX("+rotX+"deg)
        rotateY(0deg) rotateZ(0deg)";
      }

      var fingers = {};
      var spheres = {};
      Leap.loop(function(frame) {
        var seenFingers = {};
        var handIds = {};
        if (frame.hands === undefined ) {
          var handsLength = 0
        } else {
          var handsLength = frame.hands.length;
        }

        for (var handId = 0, handCount = handsLength; handId != handCount;
        handId++) {
          var hand = frame.hands[handId];
          var posX = (hand.palmPosition[0]*3);
          var posY = (hand.palmPosition[2]*3)-200;
          var posZ = (hand.palmPosition[1]*3)-400;
          var rotX = (hand._rotation[2]*90);
          var rotY = (hand._rotation[1]*90);
          var rotZ = (hand._rotation[0]*90);
          var sphere = spheres[hand.id];
          if (!sphere) {
            var sphereDiv = document.getElementById("sphere").cloneNode(true);
            sphereDiv.setAttribute('id',hand.id);
            sphereDiv.style.backgroundColor='#'+Math.floor(Math.
            random()*16777215).toString(16);
            document.getElementById('scene').appendChild(sphereDiv);
            spheres[hand.id] = hand.id;
```

149

```
      } else {
        var sphereDiv = document.getElementById(hand.id);
        if (typeof(sphereDiv) != 'undefined' && sphereDiv != null) {
          moveSphere(sphereDiv, posX, posY, posZ, rotX, rotY, rotZ);
        }
      }
      handIds[hand.id] = true;
    }
    for (handId in spheres) {
      if (!handIds[handId]) {
        var sphereDiv = document.getElementById(spheres[handId]);
        sphereDiv.parentNode.removeChild(sphereDiv);
        delete spheres[handId];
      }
    }

    for (var pointableId = 0, pointableCount = frame.pointables.length;
    pointableId != pointableCount; pointableId++) {
      var pointable = frame.pointables[pointableId];
      var newFinger = false;
      if (pointable.finger) {
        if (!fingers[pointable.id]) {
          fingers[pointable.id] = [];
          newFinger = true;
        }

        for (var partId = 0, length; partId != 4; partId++) {
          var posX = (pointable.positions[partId][0]*3);
          var posY = (pointable.positions[partId][2]*3)-200;
          var posZ = (pointable.positions[partId][1]*3)-400;

          var id = pointable.id+'_'+partId;

          var finger = fingers[id];
          if (newFinger) {
            var fingerDiv = document.getElementById("finger").
            cloneNode(true);
            fingerDiv.setAttribute('id', id);
            fingerDiv.style.backgroundColor='#'+Math.floor(pointable.
            type*500).toString(16);
            document.getElementById('scene').appendChild(fingerDiv);
            fingers[pointable.id].push(id);
          } else {
            var fingerDiv = document.getElementById(id);
            if (typeof(fingerDiv) != 'undefined' && fingerDiv != null) {
              moveFinger(fingerDiv, posX, posY, posZ);
            }
          }
        }
```

```
          seenFingers[pointable.id] = true;
        }

        //var dirX = -(pointable.direction[1]*90);
        //var dirY = -(pointable.direction[2]*90);
        //var dirZ = (pointable.direction[0]*90);
      }
    }
    for (var fingerId in fingers) {
      if (!seenFingers[fingerId]) {
        var ids = fingers[fingerId];
        for (var index in ids) {
          var fingerDiv = document.getElementById(ids[index]);
          fingerDiv.parentNode.removeChild(fingerDiv);
        }
        delete fingers[fingerId];
      }
    }
    document.getElementById('showHands').addEventListener('mousedown',
    function() {
      document.getElementById('app').setAttribute('class','show-hands');
    }, false);
    document.getElementById('hideHands').addEventListener('mousedown',
    function() {
      document.getElementById('app').setAttribute('class','');
    }, false);
  });

</script>
<style>
  *,*:before,*:after {
    margin: 0;
    padding: 0;
    border: 0;
    -webkit-box-sizing: border-box;
    -moz-box-sizing: border-box;
    box-sizing: border-box;
  }
  button {
    padding: .5em;
  }
  #app {
    position: absolute;
    width: 100%;
    height: 100%;
    font-size: 200%;
    overflow: hidden;
```

```
  background-color: #101010;
  -webkit-perspective: 1000;
}
#scene,
#scene:before {
  position: absolute;
  left: 50%;
  top: 50%;
  width: 40em;
  height: 40em;
  margin: -20em 0 0 -20em;
  border: 4px solid #A0A0A0;
  background-color: rgba(255,255,255,.1);
  background-image:
  -webkit-linear-gradient(rgba(255,255,255,.4) .1em, transparent .1em),
  -webkit-linear-gradient(0deg, rgba(255,255,255,.4) .1em, transparent .1em),
  -webkit-linear-gradient(rgba(255,255,255,.3) .05em, transparent .05em),
  -webkit-linear-gradient(0deg, rgba(255,255,255,.3) .05em,
  transparent .05em);
  background-size: 5em 5em, 5em 5em, 1em 1em, 1em 1em;
  background-position: -.1em -.1em, -.1em -.1em, -.05em -.05em, -.05em
  -.05em;
  transform-style: preserve-3d;
  -moz-transform-style: preserve-3d;
  -webkit-transform-style: preserve-3d;
  transform: rotateX(75deg);
  -moz-transform: rotateX(75deg);
  -webkit-transform: rotateX(75deg);
}
#scene {
  transform: rotateX(75deg);
  -moz-transform: rotateX(75deg);
  -webkit-transform: rotateX(75deg);
}
#scene:before {
  content: '';
  transform: rotateX(90deg) translateZ(19.5em) translateY(20em);
  -moz-transform: rotateX(90deg) translateZ(19.5em) translateY(20em);
  -webkit-transform: rotateX(90deg) translateZ(19.5em) translateY(20em);
}
.cube {
  background-color: red;
  transform-style: preserve-3d;
  -moz-transform-style: preserve-3d;
  -webkit-transform-style: preserve-3d;
  transform: translateX(19.5em) translateY(19.5em) translateZ(0em);
  -moz-transform: translateX(19.5em) translateY(19.5em) translateZ(0em);
```

```
  -webkit-transform: translateX(19.5em) translateY(19.5em)
   translateZ(0em);
}
.finger,
.sphere {
  position: absolute;
  left: 50%;
  top: 50%;
  width: 1em;
  height: 1em;
  margin: -.5em 0 0 -.5em;
  -webkit-transform-style: preserve-3d;
  -moz-transform-style: preserve-3d;
  transform-style: preserve-3d;
  -webkit-transform: translateX(14.5em) translateY(14.5em) translateZ(0);
  -moz-transform: translateX(14.5em) translateY(14.5em) translateZ(0);
  transform: translateX(14.5em) translateY(14.5em) translateZ(0);
}

.finger {
  opacity: .8;
}

.sphere {
  opacity: .3;
  display: none;
  font-size: 100px;
}

.show-hands .sphere {
  display: block;
}

.face {
  position: absolute;
  width: 1em;
  height: 1em;
  background-color: inherit;
  -webkit-transform-style: preserve-3d;
  -moz-transform-style: preserve-3d;
  transform-style: preserve-3d;
  -webkit-transform-origin: 0 0;
  -moz-transform-origin: 0 0;
  transform-origin: 0 0;
  -webkit-box-shadow: inset 0 0 0 1px rgba(255,255,255,.9);
  -moz-box-shadow: inset 0 0 0 1px rgba(255,255,255,.9);
  box-shadow: inset 0 0 0 1px rgba(255,255,255,.9);
}
```

```css
.cube .face.tp {
  -webkit-transform: translateZ(1em);
  -moz-transform: translateZ(1em);
  transform: translateZ(1em);
}
.cube .face.ft {
  -webkit-transform: rotateX(90deg) translateZ(-1em);
  -moz-transform: rotateX(90deg) translateZ(-1em);
  transform: rotateX(90deg) translateZ(-1em);
}
.cube .face.bk {
  -webkit-transform: rotateX(90deg);
  -moz-transform: rotateX(90deg);
  transform: rotateX(90deg);
}
.cube .face.lt {
  -webkit-transform: rotateY(90deg) translateX(-1em);
  -moz-transform: rotateY(90deg) translateX(-1em);
  transform: rotateY(90deg) translateX(-1em);
}
.cube .face.rt {
  -webkit-transform: rotateY(90deg) translateX(-1em) translateZ(1em);
  -moz-transform: rotateY(90deg) translateX(-1em) translateZ(1em);
  transform: rotateY(90deg) translateX(-1em) translateZ(1em);
}

.finger .face.tp {
  -webkit-transform: translateZ(1em);
  -moz-transform: translateZ(1em);
  transform: translateZ(1em);
  height: 3em;
}
.finger .face.ft {
  -webkit-transform: rotateX(90deg) translateZ(-3em);
  -moz-transform: rotateX(90deg) translateZ(-3em);
  transform: rotateX(90deg) translateZ(-3em);
}
.finger .face.bk {
  -webkit-transform: rotateX(90deg);
  -moz-transform: rotateX(90deg);
  transform: rotateX(90deg);
}
.finger .face.lt {
  -webkit-transform: rotateY(90deg) translateX(-1em);
  -moz-transform: rotateY(90deg) translateX(-1em);
  transform: rotateY(90deg) translateX(-1em);
  height: 3em;
}
```

```css
.finger .face.rt {
  -webkit-transform: rotateY(90deg) translateX(-1em) translateZ(1em);
  -moz-transform: rotateY(90deg) translateX(-1em) translateZ(1em);
  transform: rotateY(90deg) translateX(-1em) translateZ(1em);
  height: 3em;
}

</style>
</head>
<body>
  <div id="app" class="show-hands">
    <button id="showHands">Show Hands</button>
    <button id="hideHands">hide Hands</button>
    <div id="scene">
      <div id="cube" class="cube">
        <div class="face tp"></div>
        <div class="face lt"></div>
        <div class="face rt"></div>
        <div class="face ft"></div>
        <div class="face bk"></div>
      </div>
      <div id="finger" class="cube finger">
        <div class="face tp"></div>
        <div class="face lt"></div>
        <div class="face rt"></div>
        <div class="face ft"></div>
        <div class="face bk"></div>
      </div>
      <div id="sphere" class="cube sphere">
        <div class="face tp"></div>
        <div class="face lt"></div>
        <div class="face rt"></div>
        <div class="face ft"></div>
        <div class="face bk"></div>
      </div>
    </div>
  </div>
</body>
</html>
```

The output of the app is a visualization of your hand as recognized by Leap Motion (Figure 9-4).

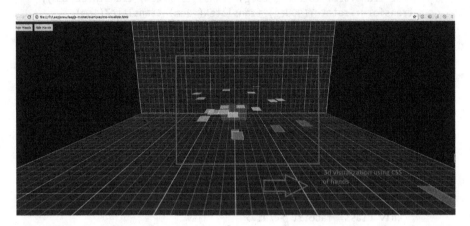

*Figure 9-4.* *CSS Visualizer*

# Using ThreeJS

In the next example we use the ThreeJS library. This very useful WebGL library can create very good graphic-enabled applications for the web. The ThreeJS library is available from the link at https://threejs.org/.

Let's use ThreeJS with Leap Motion. We will have to use necessary libraries for ThreeJS and with it add the Leap Motion JS library.

We will be implementing WebGL with ThreeJS using the LeapJS framework.

First let us see how a scene is rendered in ThreeJS (Figure 9-5).

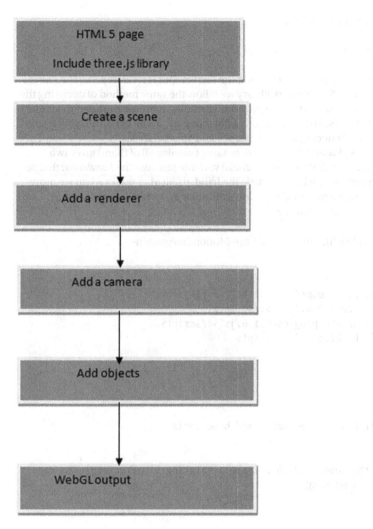

**Figure 9-5.** *ThreeJS scene flow*

In the HTML5 page we add the Three.js library. Now in the init() method we declare the variables that we will be using in our scene. The code creates a scene as follows:

```
scene = new THREE.Scene();
```

After that we create a scene renderer object with this statement:

```
Renderer = new THREE.Canvasrenderer;
```

A camera object is created next:

```
camera = new THREE.PerspectiveCamera();
```

Finally we add mesh and geometry, and the final output is rendered.

As we add the LeapJS framework library we follow the same method of declaring the `Leap.loop` function as described in the previous example, where we captured the frame data for hands and fingers. The GUI output of obtaining the frame and displaying it is handled by the variables declared as bonemeshes and jointmeshes.

Using the LeapJS plugins (the github download contains all of them) gives two entries, handHold and handEntry. The handHold variable provides the *handdata;* that is, frame-by-frame coordinates when we move the hand. HandEntry tracks when we move the hand within the range of the LeapMotion Controller and when it is out of range.

The code is shown in Listing 9-3.

***Listing 9-3.*** The Code with ThreeJS and Leap Motion Integration

```
<html>
<head>
  <title>Bone Hands - Leap</title>
  <script src="../leap-0.6.4.js"></script>
  <script src="lib/leap-plugins-0.1.6.js"></script>
  <script src="lib/three.js"></script>

</head>
<body>

<p>
  Move Hand over Leap to see bones and bone basis.
</p>
<p>
  Even without the leap, you should see a rotating blue rectangle to know
that your WebGL is working.
</p>

</body>

<script>
// note: before implementing based off of this, you can instead grab the
boneHand plugin, which does this all for you,
// better than the way it is done here.
// https://developer.leapmotion.com/gallery/bone-hands
// If you prefer to see exactly how it all works, read on..

  var colors = [0xff0000, 0x00ff00, 0x0000ff];
  var baseBoneRotation = (new THREE.Quaternion).setFromEuler(
      new THREE.Euler(Math.PI / 2, 0, 0)
  );
```

```javascript
Leap.loop({background: true}, {
  hand: function (hand) {

    hand.fingers.forEach(function (finger) {

      // This is the meat of the example - Positioning `the cylinders on
        every frame:
      finger.data('boneMeshes').forEach(function(mesh, i){
        var bone = finger.bones[i];

        mesh.position.fromArray(bone.center());

        mesh.setRotationFromMatrix(
          (new THREE.Matrix4).fromArray( bone.matrix() )
        );

        mesh.quaternion.multiply(baseBoneRotation);
      });

      finger.data('jointMeshes').forEach(function(mesh, i){
        var bone = finger.bones[i];

        if (bone) {
          mesh.position.fromArray(bone.prevJoint);
        }else{
          // special case for the finger tip joint sphere:
          bone = finger.bones[i-1];
          mesh.position.fromArray(bone.nextJoint);
        }

      });

    });

    var armMesh = hand.data('armMesh');

    armMesh.position.fromArray(hand.arm.center());

    armMesh.setRotationFromMatrix(
      (new THREE.Matrix4).fromArray( hand.arm.matrix() )
    );

    armMesh.quaternion.multiply(baseBoneRotation);

    armMesh.scale.x = hand.arm.width / 2;
    armMesh.scale.z = hand.arm.width / 4;
```

```javascript
      renderer.render(scene, camera);

}})
  // these two LeapJS plugins, handHold and handEntry are available from
      leapjs-plugins, included above.
  // handHold provides hand.data
  // handEntry provides handFound/handLost events.
.use('handHold')
.use('handEntry')
.on('handFound', function(hand){

  hand.fingers.forEach(function (finger) {

    var boneMeshes = [];
    var jointMeshes = [];

    finger.bones.forEach(function(bone) {

      // create joints

      // CylinderGeometry(radiusTop, radiusBottom, height, radiusSegments,
          heightSegments, openEnded)
      var boneMesh = new THREE.Mesh(
          new THREE.CylinderGeometry(5, 5, bone.length),
          new THREE.MeshPhongMaterial()
      );

      boneMesh.material.color.setHex(0xffffff);
      scene.add(boneMesh);
      boneMeshes.push(boneMesh);
    });

    for (var i = 0; i < finger.bones.length + 1; i++) {

      var jointMesh = new THREE.Mesh(
          new THREE.SphereGeometry(8),
          new THREE.MeshPhongMaterial()
      );

      jointMesh.material.color.setHex(0x0088ce);
      scene.add(jointMesh);
      jointMeshes.push(jointMesh);

    }
```

```javascript
    finger.data('boneMeshes', boneMeshes);
    finger.data('jointMeshes', jointMeshes);

  });

  if (hand.arm){ // 2.0.3+ have arm api,
    // CylinderGeometry(radiusTop, radiusBottom, height, radiusSegments,
      heightSegments, openEnded)
    var armMesh = new THREE.Mesh(
      new THREE.CylinderGeometry(1, 1, hand.arm.length, 64),
      new THREE.MeshPhongMaterial()
    );

    armMesh.material.color.setHex(0xffffff);

    scene.add(armMesh);

    hand.data('armMesh', armMesh);

  }

})
.on('handLost', function(hand){

  hand.fingers.forEach(function (finger) {

    var boneMeshes = finger.data('boneMeshes');
    var jointMeshes = finger.data('jointMeshes');

    boneMeshes.forEach(function(mesh){
      scene.remove(mesh);
    });

    jointMeshes.forEach(function(mesh){
      scene.remove(mesh);
    });

    finger.data({
      boneMeshes: null,
      boneMeshes: null
    });

  });
```

```javascript
  var armMesh = hand.data('armMesh');
  scene.remove(armMesh);
  hand.data('armMesh', null);

  renderer.render(scene, camera);

})
.connect();

// all units in mm
var initScene = function () {
  window.scene = new THREE.Scene();
  window.renderer = new THREE.WebGLRenderer({
    alpha: true
  });

  window.renderer.setClearColor(0x000000, 0);
  window.renderer.setSize(window.innerWidth, window.innerHeight);

  window.renderer.domElement.style.position = 'fixed';
  window.renderer.domElement.style.top = 0;
  window.renderer.domElement.style.left = 0;
  window.renderer.domElement.style.width = '100%';
  window.renderer.domElement.style.height = '100%';

  document.body.appendChild(window.renderer.domElement);

  var directionalLight = new THREE.DirectionalLight( 0xffffff, 1 );
  directionalLight.position.set( 0, 0.5, 1 );
  window.scene.add(directionalLight);

  window.camera = new THREE.PerspectiveCamera(45, window.innerWidth /
  window.innerHeight, 1, 1000);
  window.camera.position.fromArray([0, 100, 500]);
  window.camera.lookAt(new THREE.Vector3(0, 160, 0));

  window.addEventListener('resize', function () {

    camera.aspect = window.innerWidth / window.innerHeight;
    camera.updateProjectionMatrix();
    renderer.setSize(window.innerWidth, window.innerHeight);
    renderer.render(scene, camera);

  }, false);

  scene.add(camera);

  var geometry = new THREE.CubeGeometry(30, 45, 10);
```

```
    var material = new THREE.MeshPhongMaterial({color: 0x0000cc});
    window.cube = new THREE.Mesh(geometry, material);
    cube.position.set(0,0,0);
    cube.castShadow = true;
    cube.receiveShadow = true;
    scene.add(cube);

    renderer.render(scene, camera);
  };

  initScene();

  var rotateCube = function(){
    cube.rotation.x += 0.01;
    cube.rotation.y += 0.02;
    renderer.render(scene, camera);

    window.requestAnimationFrame(rotateCube);
  };

  rotateCube();

</script>
</html>
```

The output for the app is shown in Figure 9-6. It tracks our hand with cool 3D graphics.

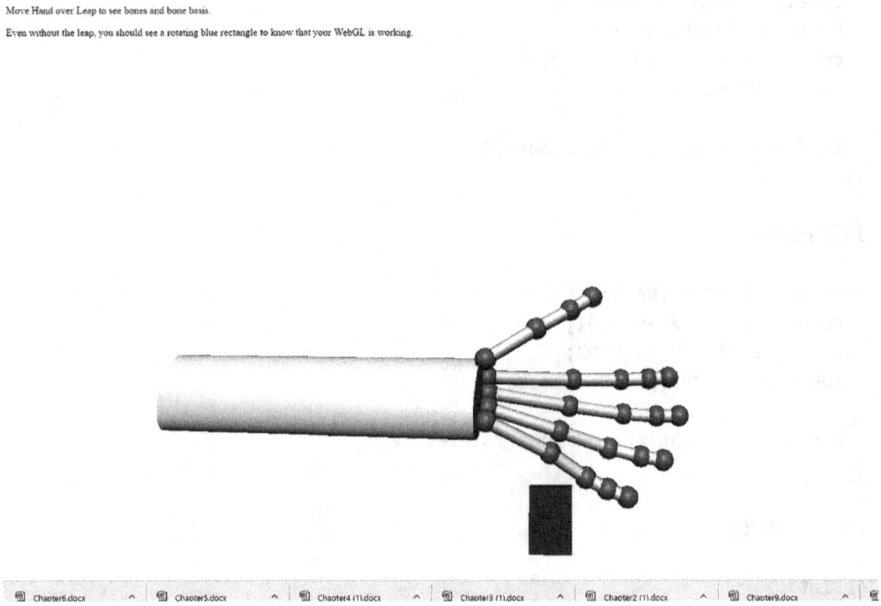

*Figure 9-6.* *ThreeJS implementation with Leap Motion*

# Windows 10 UWP and the Leap Motion Controller

In this last section we will implement Leap Motion with the Windows 10 Universal Windows Platform (UWP). We will use the LeapCursorJS framework for our implementation. We will use Windows 10 UWP JavaScript template for our work.

Let's Start. First you need to download the LeapCursor.js framework from github (https://github.com/roboleary/LeapCursor.js).

You should now open the LeapCursor.js-master directory (Figure 9-7) and locate the leapcursor-with-dependecies.min.js file. Later you will copy this to the JavaScript folder of the Windows 10 UWP project you create.

Leapjsnew > LasttryWin10 > LeapCursor.js-master

| Name | Date modified | Type | Size |
|---|---|---|---|
| lib | 25-05-2015 08:58 | File folder | |
| resources | 25-05-2015 08:58 | File folder | |
| .gitattributes | 25-05-2015 08:58 | Text Document | 1 KB |
| .gitignore | 25-05-2015 08:58 | Text Document | 3 KB |
| demo.html | 25-05-2015 08:58 | Spark HTML Docu... | 4 KB |
| leapcursor.js | 25-05-2015 08:58 | JavaScript File | 20 KB |
| leapcursor.min.js | 25-05-2015 08:58 | JavaScript File | 13 KB |
| leapcursor-with-dependencies.min.js | 25-05-2015 08:58 | JavaScript File | 509 KB |
| leapcursor-with-dependencies-embedde... | 25-05-2015 08:58 | JavaScript File | 502 KB |
| README.md | 25-05-2015 08:58 | MD File | 7 KB |

***Figure 9-7.*** *Copy the required library*

Open Visual Studio 2015 and extend the WinJS App template (Figure 9-8).

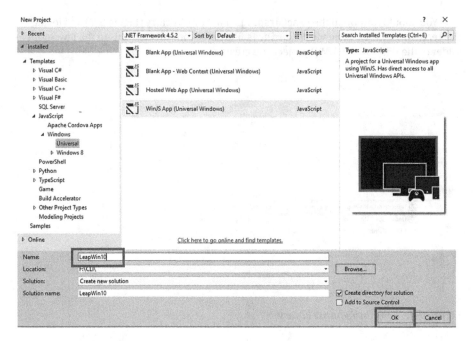

**Figure 9-8.** *Name the project*

In the next screen, target the build and keep it as it is (Figure 9-9).

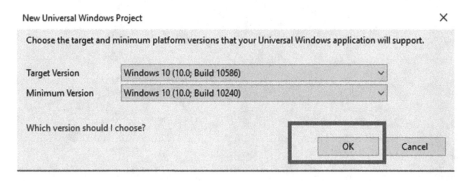

**Figure 9-9.** *Targeting the build*

Copy the `leapcursor-with-dependencies.min.js` file (from the Leapcursor.js master) and paste it into the `js` folder (Figure 9-10).

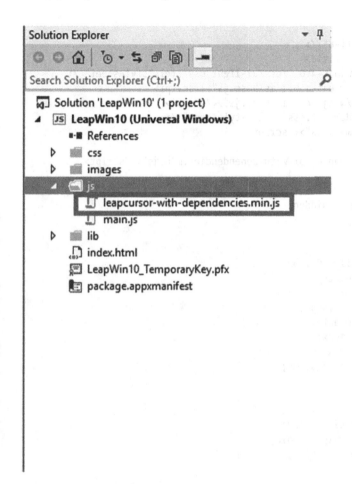

*Figure 9-10. Copying the Leap cursor JS library*

Listing 9-4 shows the coding logic in the `index.html` page. Note how we implement the Leap cursor by including the following dependency:

```
<script src="/path/to/leapcursor-with-dependencies.min.js"></script>
```

Thanks to this include you will see a hand cursor that navigates through the canvas window. The JS file is integrated with the ThreeJS implementation so that the Leap Motion cursor that is generated will have a good GUI base.

The function `bind` listens for the Leap Motion hand tracking that acts like a mouse cursor.

***Listing 9-4.*** The code for UWP Leap logic

```
!DOCTYPE html>
<html>
<head>
    <meta charset="utf-8" />
    <title>LeapWin10</title>
    <link href="lib/winjs-4.0.1/css/ui-light.css" rel="stylesheet" />
    <script src="lib/winjs-4.0.1/js/base.js"></script>
    <script src="lib/winjs-4.0.1/js/ui.js"></script>
    <link href="css/default.css" rel="stylesheet" />
    <script src="js/main.js"></script>

    <script src="js/leapcursor-with-dependencies.min.js"></script>
    <style>
        body {
            overflow-x: hidden;
        }

        p {
            font-family: Calibri;
            font-size: 25px;
            width: 60%;
            max-width: 750px;
            margin: 0 auto;
            padding: 10px;
            border: 10px solid #FFF;
            text-align: justify;
        }

            p.title {
                font-size: 50px;
                font-weight: bold;
                color: #6DCC44;
            }

            p a {
                font-weight: bold;
                color: #FFF;
                text-decoration: none;
                background: #47B6E0;
            }
```

```css
        #click-notice {
            display: none;
            width: 550px;
            height: 580px;
            position: absolute;
            color: #6DCC44;
        }

        #click-notice .handlebar {
            float: left;
            font-size: 480px;
            line-height: 480px;
            font-family: Times New Roman;
        }

        #click-notice .notice {
            float: left;
            margin-top: 240px;
            padding: 10px;
            margin-left: -30px;
            background: #6DCC44;
            color: #FFF;
            font-size: 80px;
            line-height: 80px;
        }
    </style>

</head>
<body class="win-type-body">
    <script>

                /**
                 *
                 */
                function bind(elm, evt, f) {

                        if (elm.addEventListener) { elm.
                        addEventListener(evt, f, false);

                        } else if (elm.attachEvent) { elm.attachEvent('on' +
                          evt, f); }
                }

    </script>
    <div id="click-notice"><div class="handlebar">}</div><div
class="notice">CLICK!</div></div>
</body>
</html>
```

The output for the app behaves as if you are using Hand gesture to control the movement (Figure 9-11). It uses Leap Motion tracking with Windows 10 UWP.

*Figure 9-11.* *The Leap cursor*

Let's now have some fun with the cursor; let's increase its size. The following line of code will change it accordingly:

```
<scriptsrc="js/leapcursor-with-dependencies.min.js?color=#00ffff&width=1024&height=768"></script>
```

The output is shown in Figure 9-12.

**Figure 9-12.** *The giant sized cursor*

# Summary

In this chapter we got you started integrating JavaScript and the Leap Motion Controller. In our code example we used the ThreeJS platform with Leap Motion to get the best graphics. We then integrated Leap Motion with the Windows 10 UWP.

This entire book has been a journey in extending Leap Motion to a variety of programming languages and platforms, and along the way we tried out some examples showing various use cases. You can take it further on your own by extending the applications to suit your preferences.

# Index

© Abhishek Nandy 2016
A. Nandy, *Leap Motion for Developers*, DOI 10.1007/978-1-4842-2550-9

# Get the eBook for only $4.99!

Why limit yourself?

Now you can take the weightless companion with you wherever you go and access your content on your PC, phone, tablet, or reader.

Since you've purchased this print book, we are happy to offer you the eBook for just $4.99.

Convenient and fully searchable, the PDF version enables you to easily find and copy code—or perform examples by quickly toggling between instructions and applications.

To learn more, go to http://www.apress.com/us/shop/companion or contact support@apress.com.

Printed in the United States
By Bookmasters